FERGUSON
CAREER BIOGRAPHIES

WILLIAM H.
REHNQUIST

Chief Justice of the
U.S. Supreme Court

Scott Cameron

Ferguson
An imprint of ☑®Facts On File

William H. Rehnquist: Chief Justice of the U.S. Supreme Court

Ferguson
An imprint of Facts On File, Inc.
132 West 31st Street
New York NY 10001

Library of Congress Cataloging-in-Publication Data
Cameron, Scott.
  William H. Rehnquist : Chief Justice of the U.S. Supreme Court / Scott Cameron.
      p. cm.
  Includes bibliographical references and index.
  ISBN 0-8160-5888-1 (hc : alk. paper)
  1. Rehnquist, William H., 1924- 2. Judges—United States—Biography. [1. United States. Supreme Court—Biography.] I. Title.
  KF8745.R44C36   2005
  347.73'2634—dc22

                                                              2004008820

Ferguson books are available at special discounts when purchased in bulk quantities for businesses, associations, institutions, or sales promotions. Please call our Special Sales Department in New York at (212) 967-8800 or (800) 322-8755.

You can find Ferguson on the World Wide Web at http://www.fergpubco.com

Text design by David Strelecky

Pages 109–129 adapted from Ferguson's *Encyclopedia of Careers and Vocational Guidance, Twelfth Edition.*

Printed in the United States of America

MP TB 10 9 8 7 6 5 4 3 2 1

This book is printed on acid-free paper.

CONTENTS

1

THE INTERVIEW OF A LIFETIME

In the summer of 1951, William H. Rehnquist was one of the top students at Stanford Law School in California. Like many of his classmates, he wanted to be a clerk for a Supreme Court justice—a prestigious yearlong position that usually helps launch a successful legal career. Rehnquist knew that the first step was landing an interview in Washington, D.C. At that time, however, cross-country flights were very expensive. The idea of taking the train all the way from California to Washington, D.C. just for an interview seemed slightly insane.

Fortunately, the Supreme Court came to Stanford. Or at least, one of its justices did. Robert H. Jackson, a well-respected justice on the Court, was invited to campus to dedicate the law school's new building. While at

Stanford, Justice Jackson planned to visit some old colleagues. One of these colleagues was his former Supreme Court law clerk, Phil Neal, who was now a law professor at Stanford. When Professor Neal heard that Justice Jackson was looking for a new law clerk, he thought of William "Bill" Rehnquist. By that time, Rehnquist was well known on campus for his brilliant debating skills and his keen understanding of the law. So, shortly before Justice Jackson's visit, Professor Neal asked Rehnquist if he would like to interview to be a clerk for Justice Jackson.

Rehnquist was surprised by the offer, and he eagerly accepted it.

A Cold Drive into Sunshine

Professor Neal set up the interview in a faculty office at the law school. Rehnquist was impressed—and relieved—by how informal Justice Jackson was, and he quickly relaxed. The first few questions were predictable. First, the justice asked Rehnquist about his background, including the three years he had spent in the Air Force during World War II. Next he asked about Rehnquist's coursework at Stanford. But then came a surprising question. The justice asked if the name Rehnquist was Swedish. The startled law student said it was. Justice Jackson then told some stories about some Swedish clients he had worked for back in New York, before becoming a justice. Rehnquist listened attentively, but as he later noted, "I felt I should be doing more to make a favorable impression on him." But there was no opportunity to do so. After finishing his stories, the justice thanked Rehnquist for the interview, shook his hand, and sent him on his way. Years later, Rehnquist said, "I walked out of the room convinced that he had written me off as a total loss in the first minutes of our visit." Rehnquist was wrong. In November, Justice Jackson sent a letter saying that he needed assistance in his office. Although he already had one clerk, there was too much work for one person. He asked Rehnquist to come to Washington and serve as a clerk for 18 months, beginning on February 1, 1952. "Delighted by this quite unexpected offer, I accepted it immediately," Rehnquist later wrote.

After graduating from Stanford Law School a few months later, Rehnquist drove east to Washington, D.C. He drove a blue 1941 Studebaker, which was loaded with all his possessions. It was winter, and most of the country was bitterly cold—which was unfortunate, since the Studebaker did not have any heat. However, during the last 40 miles of the drive, the sun broke through the gray clouds. Rehnquist later wrote about the experience: "I had the feeling that it was personally welcoming me to the Nation's Capital."

William Rehnquist's job as a U.S. Supreme Court law clerk was just the beginning of a long and prestigious career. (Landov)

Rehnquist drove directly to his great-aunt's house in northwest Washington. After a day of getting acquainted with the city, he reported to work at the Supreme Court.

He stood before the entrance and marveled at the building, which he once wrote looked like "a magnificent Greek temple of white marble." He admired the 16 Corinthian marble columns, and the famous inscription above them: "Equal Justice Under Law."

Then William H. Rehnquist climbed the Supreme Court steps for the first time. He surely had little idea that, more than 30 years later, he would sit in the Court's most powerful position, chief justice.

The Last Word

For a law school graduate like Rehnquist, working as a Supreme Court clerk was like another year of education. By assisting one of the court's nine justices, he would be able to see how the Court works.

The Supreme Court is the highest court in the United States. For people who are not satisfied with court rulings in their states or in lower courts, the Supreme Court is the last chance for a different ruling. The Supreme Court has the last word.

The Court consists of one chief justice and eight associate justices. All the justices have law degrees and have worked as lawyers, but they come from a variety of backgrounds. Some have been judges in lower courts. Others have been attorneys in private practice. Some justices have spent a good deal of their careers working in government.

All nine justices have equal power. They are guaranteed their positions for the rest of their lives. When a justice retires or dies, the current president of the United States nominates a new justice. The Senate then decides whether to confirm, or approve, the nominee. If the majority of senators thinks that the nominee should not become a justice, the president has to nominate someone else.

Because the justices hold lifelong positions, they do not have to worry about political pressure. Even if they make decisions that the president and Congress do not like, the justices cannot be fired. (If a justice abuses his or her power and acts unethically, Congress may remove the justice, but this has never happened.)

It usually takes many months or years for a case to get to the Supreme Court. The first part of this long process occurs when a case is heard, or presented, in a lower court. This lower court may be a state court or a federal court. After the court makes a ruling, the "losing" party can appeal. This means that the case could be brought to a higher court for review, in the hope that the higher court will make a different ruling. This process continues, so that the case is heard at higher and higher levels. The last level is the Supreme Court.

Each year, lawyers around the country send thousands of new cases to the Court. They want the justices to review their case and, hopefully, issue a new ruling. The Court cannot possibly accept all of these cases. As a result, the justices and their clerks have to read all the cases and decide which ones are the most important. The justices take this work very seriously. Once they make a decision, all the other courts in the country have to follow it. Sometimes, the Court's decisions are not popular with the public, but the government still has to obey the ruling.

The Court relies on two things when making its decisions: the U.S. Constitution and the laws passed by Congress. Because the Constitution was written more than 200 years ago, there are many societal and legal issues it does not directly address. In the same way, laws made in Congress often do not address every possible issue. As a result, the justices have to interpret the Constitution and the laws passed by Congress. Often, not all of the nine justices have the same interpretation, so they do not reach a unanimous decision. Some justices vote in favor of the plaintiff—the person or group who brought the case to the Court—and others vote in favor of the defendant. Because there are nine justices, there is never a tie. The "side" that gets the most votes is the side that wins the case.

The U.S. Supreme Court building, home of the highest court in the United States. (Landov)

To see this grand old legal system up close was a golden opportunity for the young William Rehnquist. Given how his career developed, it seems clear that he made the most of that opportunity.

2

FROM GI TO TOP OF THE CLASS

On October 1, 1924, William Hubbs Rehnquist was born in Shorewood, Wisconsin, a suburb of Milwaukee. He lived with his sister, Jean, and his parents in a tan brick house. His father, William Benjamin Rehnquist, was a first-generation American whose parents had come from Sweden. As a wholesale paper salesman, William B. Rehnquist was able to provide a comfortable, middle-class home for his family. William Jr.'s mother, Margery, was fluent in five languages. She worked as a freelance translator for several Milwaukee companies. Margery had graduated from the University of Wisconsin and participated in civic activities.

The Rehnquist household was staunchly Republican. This was an important and long-lasting factor in William's political development. In the Rehnquist home, dinner time

9

was often a forum for political conversations. The family enthusiastically supported and admired Republican leaders such as Robert Taft and Herbert Hoover.

William began elementary school in the late 1920s, right at the start of the Great Depression. It was an extremely difficult time for the United States. After the stock market crash of 1929, banks cut back their loans to businesses. In turn, the businesses cut back their production. As a result, the country went into a 10-year depression that left millions of Americans jobless and very poor.

By 1932, when William was still in elementary school, the country was in bad shape. Many Americans blamed the Depression on President Herbert Hoover, a Republican. That year, there was a presidential election. Anxious for a change, the nation elected Franklin Delano Roosevelt, a Democrat. Hoover's defeat was a huge disappointment to the Rehnquist family; they did not agree with Roosevelt's policies. When one of William's elementary school teachers asked him what he wanted to do when he grew up, he said, "I'm going to change the government."

In high school, William advocated another kind of change. As the features editor of his high school newspaper, William wrote commentaries. In these columns, he criticized famous commentators who injected their own opinions and interpretations into their news reports. He

The defeat of Republican president Herbert Hoover (pictured here) by Democrat Franklin Delano Roosevelt was a huge disappointment for the Rehnquist family. (Landov)

felt strongly that news should be only fact and not opinion. "The recent windy weather," he wrote, "may not have been due entirely to weather conditions. Some of the self-styled news 'interpreters' have been doing a little too much spouting of their own. There is no fault to be found with straight news broadcasts; they perform a valuable service. But thorns to the 'commentators.'" In commentaries such as this, it is possible to see William's political development: Years later, he criticized some judges for using their own opinions to interpret the law.

The War

During William's teenage years, the news was filled with grave reports of the war in Europe. This war would later become known as World War II. On December 7, 1941, while Rehnquist was at his girlfriend's house, Japan attacked the United States at Pearl Harbor, Hawaii. This initiated U.S. involvement in the war. At the time, Rehnquist was only 17. Eager to do his part to protect his country, he became a volunteer civil defense officer. These officers ranged in age and background. Some were teenagers, some were homemakers, and others were grandparents. The officers learned skills that were important in wartime, from changing tires on big trucks to learning topography—the study of the surfaces of lands. Rehnquist was in charge of a group of neighborhood block captains who had to report crimes to the police. These captains also had to report people who were avoiding the military draft so that they would not have to go to war. In the school newspaper, Rehnquist described his duty as searching for "subversive activities which might lead to the sabotaging of our national unity."

At this time, the draft age was 21. Rehnquist planned to go to college for four years; he assumed that by the time he graduated from college, he would be 21 and ready to be drafted into the military. But in 1942, Congress lowered the draft age from 21 to 18. As a result, Rehnquist had to change his plans. In the fall of 1942, he enrolled as a freshman at Kenyon College in Gambier, Ohio, but he knew that he would probably be drafted before he graduated. In a 2001 speech, he explained, "The college advisers urged students to enlist in some sort of military program which would allow you to continue some sort of college education for a while."

In March 1943, Rehnquist followed his advisers' suggestion. He chose a pre-meteorology program with the U.S. Army Air Force. This program was designed to train people to become weather forecasters, who would help the military plan its operations around the world. Courses were held at several small American colleges. Rehnquist's first stop was Denison University in Ohio, where he had to study physics and math. It was not easy. "I had a good academic record in high school," he explained in his 2001 speech to the American Meteorological Society, "but [I] had never gone beyond plane geometry and had no physics. As a result of these deficiencies, for a while I was hanging on by the skin of my teeth in this advanced program, but finally pulled myself up into the middle ranks."

Rehnquist struggled through his coursework for over a year until he completed that stage of the training. Next, he moved on to Will Rogers Field in Oklahoma City. There, he was trained as a weather observer. He learned how to make maps, create hourly weather reports, and gauge the wind's speed by using weather balloons. "I found if you got to know the forecaster on duty," Rehnquist later explained, "he would sometimes show you how he did his work."

His next stop was Carlsbad, New Mexico. When he first saw the desert, he thought, "What godforsaken country." But, Rehnquist said, "after three months there, I had come to like it, and determined that if possible someday I would come back and live in the southwest."

From New Mexico Rehnquist was sent to Texas and then Illinois. His final U.S. stop was New Jersey, where he was trained to repair and maintain weather instruments.

In the summer of 1945, Rehnquist and his fellow weather forecasters made their way to Cairo, Egypt. "For someone who had never been out of the United States before," he said, "this was a fascinating trip. And Cairo was a fascinating destination. I still have a picture of myself sitting on horseback in front of the Sphinx, with the Great Pyramids in the distance."

After Cairo, Rehnquist moved through many other parts of North Africa. He went to Tripoli, Casablanca, and Tunis. The war had ended, but the military airports in these cities were still being dismantled. Rehnquist and his fellow forecasters had to predict the weather to help with these airport projects. It wasn't until March 1946 that sergeant William H. Rehnquist arrived back in the United States. His military career was over; it was time to go back to college.

Back to School

Rehnquist was not sure where he wanted to go to college, but he did know that he did not want to live somewhere with cold winters. "I wanted to find someplace like North Africa to go to school."

As a war veteran, Rehnquist received money from the government for his education. These educational benefits were outlined in legislation passed by the U.S. Congress in 1944. This legislation was known as the GI Bill. (GI is the abbreviation for *General Issue*, a term that refers to the clothing soldiers were given during the war.) With the GI Bill's financial assistance, Rehnquist was able to attend Stanford University in California—a place known for fairly warm winters. Even then, Stanford was an expensive and very prestigious private university. When the money from the GI Bill ran out, Rehnquist got a job as the manager of the breakfast shift in the university's cafeteria. But school was expensive, so Rehnquist was forced to find additional ways to earn money. "I had so many other part-time jobs," he said, "I can't remember them all."

His childhood interest in politics influenced Rehnquist's choice of major: political science. He worked hard. By the time he graduated in 1948, he had earned two degrees: a bachelor of arts (B.A.) and a master of arts (M.A.) in political science. He was also admitted to Phi Beta Kappa, an honorary scholarship society.

But Rehnquist was not finished with his education. He next enrolled in a master's program in government at Harvard University in Cambridge, Massachusetts. After earning this second M.A. in 1950, he went straight to Stanford Law School.

Rehnquist the Conservative

In his two years at Stanford Law School, Rehnquist quickly established himself as a brilliant scholar. He became editor of the *Stanford Law Review*, the school's legal journal. In addition, he began dating a woman named Natalie Cornell, whom he would later marry.

By the time he graduated in 1952, Rehnquist was the school's top student. One of his professors called him "the outstanding student of his law school generation." Rehnquist had good company: One of his Stanford classmates was Sandra Day (O'Connor), who would go on to serve with Rehnquist on the Supreme Court and become the first woman justice of the Court.

The Stanford Law School graduating class of 1952; both William Rehnquist (back row, farthest left) and Sandra Day (O'Connor; front row, second from left) would serve together on the U.S. Supreme Court later in their careers. (Corbis)

Throughout law school, Rehnquist was well known as an effective debater of law and contemporary politics. Even then, his political beliefs were known to be extremely conservative. The term *conservative* can have different meanings, including religious meanings. But for Rehnquist, *conservative* implies several core political beliefs. First, he believes the federal government is too large and too powerful. As a result, he says, the federal government is too intrusive in the lives of individuals. He argues that states should have more power. With more power, states could pass laws appropriate to their own cultural and geographical realities.

"I'm a strong believer in pluralism," Rehnquist once said. "Don't concentrate all the power in one place. And, you know, this is partly . . . what the framers [of the Constitution] also conceived. So, it kind of is the line where political philosophy joins judicial philosophy . . . You don't want all the power in the federal government as opposed to the states."

Another aspect of Rehnquist's conservatism is a belief in judicial restraint. This legal concept demands that judges make narrow interpretations of the Constitution—that they not let their personal beliefs influence their rulings. Usually, conservative judges make decisions that reflect what they believe was the "original intent" of the Founding Fathers who wrote the Constitution—in other words, what the writers of the Constitution wanted it to mean. Judicial restraint also calls for judges to defer to legislative decisions. This means that a judge should rarely overturn a bill passed in Congress or a state legislature. Conservatism generally favors giving more power to elected officials than to elected or appointed judges.

Because Rehnquist was so conservative, it was interesting that he became a clerk for Supreme Court Justice Robert H. Jackson. Justice Jackson was a Democrat who had worked in the administration of President Franklin Delano Roosevelt. This was the same Roosevelt whom Rehnquist had disliked during elementary school. However, although Justice Jackson was a Democrat, his views were often moderate or conservative.

3

LIFE AS A CLERK

On February 1, 1952, Rehnquist reported to the Supreme Court for his first day of work. Justice Jackson invited him into his chambers. He greeted him with what Rehnquist later described as "the same affability I remembered from our meeting at Stanford." The justice told his new clerk that he would be paid a salary of $6,400 a year. Although that is very little by today's standards, in Rehnquist's words, this was "far and away the most I had ever earned in my life."

Rehnquist spent that first morning becoming familiar with his new job. He was helped in this by George Neibank, the justice's other clerk. Neibank had been working for Justice Jackson since the fall. Therefore, he was able to explain how the office operated.

Niebank told Rehnquist that he would have three main duties. First, he would have to read and edit the justice's opinions. *Opinions* are written rulings that describe the legal reasoning for the justice's decision. His second job was to edit the justice's dissents. *Dissents* are written opinions that explain why the justice voted against the majority's opinion. Finally, he would write brief summaries of petitions for *certiorari*. These petitions are requests from individuals across the country who want the Supreme Court to consider their case.

The 1953 U.S. Supreme Court. From left, seated Associate Justices Felix Frankfurter and Hugo Black, Chief Justice Earl Warren, and Associate Justices Stanley Reed and William O. Douglas. Standing: Associate Justices Tom Clark, Robert H. Jackson (for whom Rehnquist clerked), Harold H. Burton, and Sherman Minton. (Associated Press)

On that first day, Rehnquist was given a stack of about 40 of these petitions for certiorari. Approximately 1,300 of them had been filed, and they all needed to be reviewed. Neibank suggested that he and Rehnquist split the workload.

Rehnquist was overwhelmed. As part of the review for each petition, he had to advise Justice Jackson whether to accept the case. Rehnquist later wrote about his feelings that day: "This seemed like a lot of responsibility for a brand-new law clerk." He told this to George Niebank, who gave a comforting answer. "George told me that the justice felt perfectly free to disregard a recommendation with which he disagreed." Rehnquist felt even more relieved after Neibank suggested that his reviews focus on describing the case rather than on giving his opinion.

Watching the Bench

At around noon of Rehnquist's first day, George Neibank suggested that they go watch the justices in court. Rehnquist was impressed by the grand courtroom. Even the justices, he said, "seemed dwarfed by the architecture." All nine justices sat at a long table, or bench, and wore the traditional black robes. Seated at two sets of counsel tables were attorneys who would be presenting the two sides of the case that afternoon. Rehnquist later learned that the attorneys who were wearing morning coats—similar to tuxedo jackets—were representing the

United States. It has been a tradition for lawyers from the government to wear formal attire when arguing a case before the Supreme Court.

Later, Neibank took Rehnquist to the law clerks' dining room across from the cafeteria. Rehnquist was introduced to the other justices' clerks, who were debating an opinion that Justice Jackson had sent out the previous day. He felt uncomfortable as these clerks criticized Justice Jackson's opinion. In his book *The Supreme Court,* Rehnquist described his feelings that day:

> Only later did I come to realize that it would be all but impossible to assemble a more hypercritical, not to say arrogant, audience than a group of law clerks criticizing an opinion circulated by one of their employers. Their scorn—and in due time it became my scorn, too—was . . . lavished with considerable impartiality upon the products of all nine chambers of the Court.

Rehnquist was Justice Jackson's clerk for 18 months. His clerkship ended in June 1953. He has spoken and written respectfully of the justice. However, their views on politics were sometimes different.

Justice Felix Frankfurter, however, was very influential in Rehnquist's career. Justice Frankfurter was a conservative. He told the young law clerk that "conservatives as well as liberals ought to get active on the political scene."

Justice Frankfurter thought this activism would combat the liberal activism in the country.

Rehnquist followed Justice Frankfurter's advice. He decided that the best way to become active politically was to get a job in Phoenix, Arizona. In the 1950s, Phoenix was known for its conservative politics.

Political Action

After his clerkship with Justice Jackson, Rehnquist married Natalie Cornell. Natalie, who was called Nan, was his girlfriend from Stanford Law School. She had grown up in San Diego, California. They moved to Phoenix, where Rehnquist joined a private law firm.

Over the next few years, Rehnquist and his wife had three children. In 1955, their son James was born. Two years later, they had a daughter named Janet. In 1959, they had another daughter, named Nancy.

During this time, Rehnquist worked as a lawyer. He also got involved in local politics. Soon he became known in Arizona as a very bright conservative Republican. In 1957, he wrote an article for *U.S. News & World Report* in which he criticized some Supreme Court law clerks for being too liberal. He complained that these clerks were too sympathetic to Communists and that they favored federal power over state power. These views, he concluded, might be influencing which cases the Supreme Court decided to hear.

In other articles and speeches, Rehnquist attacked more than the law clerks. He also criticized some of the justices themselves. He called three justices—Earl Warren, William O. Douglas, and Hugo L. Black—"left-wing philosophers" who made "the Constitution say what they wanted it to say." People in Arizona were now paying attention to this young lawyer from Wisconsin. He became a Republican Party official and loudly opposed new legislation that he thought was too liberal. In particular, he took a stand against busing. He strongly disagreed with the state's plan to send African-American students to schools in mostly white neighborhoods. This plan was called *busing* because students were sent to school by bus. Busing was designed to integrate different races in public schools rather than keep schools segregated.

An Influential Campaigner

In 1958, Rehnquist was selected to serve as a special state prosecutor for Arizona. His job was to prosecute, or take to court, some state officials who had been accused of fraud.

But it was not until 1964 that the connections he had made in Arizona began to pay off. That year, Rehnquist was campaigning in support of the Republican presidential candidate, Senator Barry Goldwater. The field director for Goldwater's campaign was Richard (Dick) Kleindienst.

Like Rehnquist, Kleindienst was an attorney in Phoenix. The two men became friends and worked on the campaign together.

Goldwater ended up losing the election. However, in 1968, Kleindienst worked on the campaign for the new Republican presidential candidate, Richard Nixon. Rehnquist worked on that campaign, too. When Nixon won the election, he named Kleindienst as his deputy attorney general. This was good news for Rehnquist. That same year, Kleindienst selected him to be assistant attorney general for the Office of Legal Counsel in the Justice Department.

The Rehnquists were moving back to Washington.

ASSISTANT ATTORNEY GENERAL AND SUPREME COURT NOMINEE

Rehnquist spent two-and-a-half years as the assistant attorney general for the Office of Legal Counsel. Before his arrival, the people who had his job usually did not get much attention from politicians or the media. Things were different for Rehnquist, however. During his time at the Justice Department, he became known by the media and Democrats as an articulate supporter of the president's policies.

These policies were often very controversial. For example, many critics were angry when President Nixon refused to release certain government documents to the public. They were also upset by his policy of arresting large groups of nonviolent protesters against the U.S. war in Vietnam.

President Nixon—and Rehnquist—were also criticized by some Democrats and liberals for their views on crime. Both men thought that the Supreme Court was not tough enough on people accused of a crime. They believed that the Court gave too many rights to these accused men and women. President Nixon created a new law-and-order program. Critics said this program violated citizens' rights, but Rehnquist and the president thought it would reduce crime. Among other things, this program allowed police to conduct *no-knock* entries. This meant that police could enter homes and other buildings without permission. The program also allowed police to detain accused criminals before their trial and to conduct wire-tapping and electronic surveillance.

More Supreme Court Ties

In addition to supporting the president's policies, Rehnquist had other responsibilities. He also had to help select possible nominees for the Supreme Court. This was—and still is—a very serious and complicated job. When a Supreme Court justice retires or dies, the president has to nominate a replacement. This nominee must then be confirmed, or approved, by the majority of the U.S. Senate. Because of this, it is often an intensely political process. This is even truer if the majority of the Senate is not from the president's own political party.

Rehnquist was part of a five-man team that selected Supreme Court nominees. At the top was President Nixon, followed by Chief Justice Warren Burger. Chief Justice Burger made suggestions to Attorney General John Mitchell. Mitchell added names and then passed the list on to Rehnquist and to White House aide (and fellow Stanford Law School classmate) John Ehrlichman. Together, Rehnquist and Ehrlichman refined the list. One goal was to make sure that the individuals were *strict constructionists*. This meant that they believed the Constitution should be narrowly interpreted.

Of these five men, it was Rehnquist who had to do the most detailed work. He looked at the list of candidates and did research to make sure each person was somebody the White House would want to be on the Supreme Court. Next, he created a short list of candidates. Rehnquist interviewed each candidate that Attorney General Mitchell approved to see exactly what he was like in person.

Rehnquist served as assistant attorney general under President Richard Nixon (pictured above). (Associated Press)

Searching for a Strict Constructionist

In the first two years of the Nixon administration, the Democrats held the majority in the U.S. Senate. This meant that there were more Democrats than Republicans in the Senate. Therefore, if President Nixon had the opportunity to nominate a Supreme Court justice, he would have to choose someone the Democrats would support.

Soon after taking office, President Nixon had a chance to nominate a justice. But the Senate rejected two nominees in a row. Rehnquist and Kleindienst had to help the president find a suitable nominee. Finally, in 1970, they did just that. Harry Blackmun was confirmed by a unanimous vote of 94–0.

Like Rehnquist and President Nixon, Justice Blackmun was a strict constructionist. The president was so happy to have Blackmun as a justice that he made it clear to his staff that he wanted to appoint another strict constructionist to the Court when he had the chance.

The next year, 1971, Justice Hugo Black resigned from the Court. He was one of the Court's most liberal justices, and President Nixon was thrilled to be able to replace him. Justice John Harlan, a conservative, also resigned. Now Nixon had two seats to fill.

With help from Ehrlichman and Mitchell, Rehnquist made a list of six candidates. Although there were no women on the Court yet, two women were included on the list. The media got hold of this list, and soon many publications, political groups, and politicians were criticizing the choice of the six potential nominees. The consensus was that the candidates were unimpressive. The National Women's Council did not like any of them—not even the women. *Time* magazine called the list "shocking," and one influential newsman accused President Nixon of "demeaning the Court." Clearly, Rehnquist and the others on the team would have to find better candidates.

"He sure is qualified, isn't he?"

Some members of the White House staff began to consider Rehnquist himself as a potential candidate. He clearly shared the president's conservative philosophy. At age 47, he was also considered young to be a candidate. This was positive because the president wanted to appoint a justice who would be on the Court for at least 20 years. On the negative side, however, people might think Rehnquist was not experienced enough for the Supreme Court.

There were other problems. Rehnquist was more conservative than most senators. The White House thought that this might make Rehnquist's confirmation difficult. Another problem was that Rehnquist was neither a woman nor a Southerner, and these were two groups that the president wanted to please. If he nominated Rehnquist, he might lose the support of one or both of these groups.

President Nixon tape-recorded almost all the conversations he had in the White House, so there is a record of his conversations about appointing Rehnquist. The excerpts from these conversations give an insider's view into the president's decision process. The conversation below is between the president and White House special counsel Dick Moore about Rehnquist:

> Nixon: They're just going to say he's not qualified. I mean, they're just going to say . . . he's a young fellow.
> Moore: He's the most conservative, so—

Nixon: I know he's conservative. I know all that. He'd be a fine member of the Court, but how . . . could you just put a guy who's an assistant attorney general on the Court?

Moore: Mr. President, he was second in his class at Stanford.

[Moore was incorrect; Rehnquist was actually first in his class at Stanford.]

Moore: He served as a law clerk to Robert Jackson.

Nixon: Oh, he did? Law clerk to Jackson.

Moore: To Robert H. Jackson, who you know is the cream of the crop.

Moore went on the say that Stanford was an excellent law school and that Rehnquist had worked in a well-respected law practice in Arizona.

Moore: Now he's got three years as the president's lawyer's lawyer—interpreting the statutes and the Constitution, at the Department of Justice.

Nixon: [Makes an approving sound.]

Moore: You could sell him, qualification like that. You take a Supreme Court law clerk and the fact he's a justice, it's only happened once before. It would be an impressive thing.

Later in the conversation, Moore said that Rehnquist was very bright and that he was a skilled writer and communicator. But the president still was not sure, so he talked to Rehnquist's boss, Attorney General Mitchell. He told Mitchell that after talking to Moore, he was willing to reconsider nominating Rehnquist. He asked Mitchell if he thought Rehnquist was conservative.

> Mitchell: Absolutely.
>
> Nixon: And would make a brilliant justice. Would you agree?
>
> Mitchell: Yes sir.
>
> Nixon: What would the country say about him? He sure is qualified, isn't he?
>
> Mitchell: I would believe so. I don't think there's any question about it.

Based on these conversations, it is clear that the president was considering three important factors. First, he needed to verify that Rehnquist was a conservative. Second, he was impressed that he had been a law clerk for Justice Jackson. Third, he was impressed when he was told that Rehnquist had graduated at the top of his class at Stanford Law School.

But the president still was not sure that the young assistant attorney general was the right person for the Court. Pressure mounted in Washington for the president to announce his nominations, and finally President Nixon felt he had to make a decision.

On the morning of October 21, 1971, Rehnquist received a phone call from Attorney General Mitchell. It took him a moment to absorb what Mitchell was saying. Gradually, Rehnquist understood what was happening. In a few hours, President Nixon would announce William H. Rehnquist's nomination to the Supreme Court.

A little while later, Dick Moore sat down with the new nominee and gathered information for the president's speech. By the afternoon, William H. Rehnquist's name was all over the news.

Poll Watching

Usually, a Supreme Court nominee is *vetted*. This means that the candidate's personal and professional background is investigated. If anything controversial or embarrassing is found, the White House must decide whether to go ahead with the nomination or find somebody new.

Vetting is important because it can make the confirmation process go more smoothly. When a person is nominated, a committee of senators holds confirmation hearings. These hearings take place in the Senate. The nominee sits before the committee of 16 senators and must answer their questions. These questions are sometimes very difficult; often, senators who are unsure of the nominee's suitability for the Court will ask very specific questions about his or her past.

Rehnquist's confirmation hearings were filled with tough questions about things he had done or written in the past. This would be hard on any candidate. But in Rehnquist's case, an added disadvantage was that he had not been thoroughly vetted; the White House did not delve very far into his background. Therefore, it was unprepared for what the media would say about Rehnquist's nomination.

Articles appeared in newspapers that said Rehnquist had supported racial segregation in schools. They said that he had been against busing African-American students to schools in white neighborhoods. For this reason, some Democratic senators and civil rights groups said that Rehnquist should not be confirmed.

Other news reports focused on Rehnquist's role in elections when he was a Republican Party official in Arizona. These reports said that in 1968, Rehnquist challenged and harassed African Americans and Hispanics at the voting booths. This practice was called *poll watching*. The articles implied that Rehnquist and other Republican officials had tried to intimidate these non-white voters, who usually voted for Democrats. It was not illegal for officials to challenge a voter's identity or right to vote. Harassment, however, *was* illegal. As such, it was a serious charge.

The White House had not predicted that this would become an issue. So, when the confirmation hearings began on November 3, 1971, Rehnquist was not well prepared to answer questions about the reports.

The toughest questions came from Senator Birch Bayh of Indiana. Senator Bayh, a Democrat, asked Rehnquist about the newspaper reports. By this time, six people had come forward and said that they had witnessed Rehnquist challenging voters in 1964 and 1968. One witness said he saw Rehnquist try to make a voter take a literacy test.

Rehnquist denied that he had challenged or harassed African-American or Hispanic voters. He said that instead he had given legal advice to the people who were challenging the voters. This was perfectly legal.

The committee recommended that the entire Senate vote on whether to confirm Rehnquist. Before this vote, new charges of harassment appeared in the news. Rehnquist knew that he had to do something to prove to the Senate that he was telling the truth. He sent a letter to the Senate committee's chairman, saying that the accusations were false. The Senate committee voted again to send his nomination to the Senate. This meant that all 100 senators would get to decide Rehnquist's future.

An Old Memorandum, a New Debate

In early December, senators began to debate whether Rehnquist should be confirmed. His chances seemed very good. Most senators seemed ready to confirm him.

But then *Newsweek* magazine dropped a bombshell. It published an old memorandum that was written when Rehnquist was Justice Jackson's law clerk in 1952. This memo had Rehnquist's initials on it, and it appeared to be a memo advising Justice Jackson. The subject of the page-and-a-half memo was an old and controversial Court decision called *Plessy v. Ferguson*. It seemed to show that Rehnquist supported racial segregation. To understand why this memo was so explosive, it is helpful to understand the infamous decision.

In the 1890s, African Americans were forced to sit in different train cars than white passengers. A man named Homer Plessy sat in a "whites only" train car. Although he was seven-eighths white and one-eighth African American, the train company considered him to be African American. He was put in jail for sitting in the "whites only" car. His case, *Plessy v. Ferguson*, went to the Supreme Court. In 1896, the Court ruled against Plessy. The majority of justices said that it was legal to make African Americans sit in separate train cars. However, the cars had to be "equal" in size and comfort to the cars for whites. This ruling inspired the phrase "separate but equal."

When William Rehnquist became Justice Jackson's clerk in 1952, a new civil rights case was being considered. This case, called *Brown v. Board of Education*, challenged the "separate but equal" law. The case began when an eight-year-old African-American girl named Linda Brown wanted to go to her local school. This school was just a few blocks from her home, but it did not allow African Americans. Instead, Linda Brown had to take a long bus ride to the school for African Americans.

According to the memo that *Newsweek* published, Rehnquist wanted his boss, Justice Jackson, to vote against *Brown v. Board of Education*. The memorandum was titled "A Random Thought on the Segregation Cases." In it, Rehnquist said, "I realize that it is an unpopular and unhumanitarian position . . . but I think *Plessy v. Ferguson* was right and should be re-affirmed."

The main reason for this argument seemed to be that the Court had not had long-term success in protecting the rights of minorities. The memo said that, in the long run, the majority will always "determine what the constitutional rights of the minority are."

Despite the memo, the Supreme Court voted for *Brown v. Board of Education* in 1954. In doing so, the Court overturned *Plessy v. Ferguson.* The idea of "separate but equal" was now considered to be unconstitutional.

When *Newsweek* published the memo, politicians in Washington were shocked. The White House knew it had a big problem on its hands. Democratic Senator Birch Bayh made a speech that was very critical of the memo—and of Rehnquist. Suddenly, Rehnquist's chances of confirmation looked very poor.

Later that same day, only hours after Senator Bayh's speech, Rehnquist sent a letter to the chairman of the Senate confirmation committee. The letter said that he had written the memo at Justice Jackson's request and that it was meant to be "a rough draft" of a statement of Jackson's views, not his own views. He went on to say that the memo was not a statement of his own views. Also, Rehnquist said that he supported *Brown v. Board of Education.*

Not all of the senators were convinced that Rehnquist was telling the truth. But then a letter was sent to the Senate from Donald Cronson, a law clerk Rehnquist had worked with back in 1952. In this letter, Cronson said that he had worked on the *Brown* memo, too. "A great deal of the content [of the *Brown* memo] was the result of my suggestions," Cronson wrote. More importantly for Rehnquist, Cronson said that Justice Jackson had asked them to write two memos. The first was the famous *Brown* memo, which said that *Plessy v. Ferguson* should not be overturned. The second memo said that *Plessy v. Ferguson* should be overturned. For many Senators, Cronson's letter showed that Rehnquist had been telling the truth when he said that the memo was written because Justice Jackson had asked for it.

*President Nixon presents Rehnquist (right) with a framed
commission after Rehnquist's confirmation as a new associate
justice of the U.S. Supreme Court.* (Associated Press)

But not everyone was convinced. Justice Jackson's former secretary, Elsie Douglas, accused Rehnquist of "smearing" Jackson's reputation by saying he supported segregation. Senator Bayh wanted to start the confirmation hearings again. The majority of senators, however, wanted to confirm Rehnquist.

On December 10, 1971, the Senate voted. Although 28 senators voted against his confirmation, 68 senators voted for it. William H. Rehnquist was now a Supreme Court justice.

THE CONSERVATIVE JUSTICE

Because he had been a Supreme Court law clerk, Rehnquist was familiar with how the Court operated. In his first few weeks as a justice, however, he encountered some things he had not expected. For example, he did not realize how isolating the Court could be. Here is how he described his first visit to the Court after being confirmed as a justice: "It was kind of a gray afternoon . . . And I just felt, literally, like I'd entered a monastery." This feeling increased after his first few weeks at the Court. "When I first went on the Court," he wrote, "I was both surprised and dismayed at how little interplay there was between the various justices." Rehnquist was disappointed that most justices communicated through memos and notes, rather than through person-to-person discussion.

Each justice had a different working style. Some justices had four clerks, while others had three. Some justices had one office, but others were forced to find an additional office because their first office was not large enough. As a new justice, Rehnquist had to decide what was right for him.

In the end, he decided that he would have only three clerks instead of four. These clerks were all recent law school graduates. Like the other justices, he decided that his clerks would stay for one year. By the end of this one-year term, Rehnquist once wrote, the clerks "have worked very hard . . . and are glad to go on to something else in the profession, and I am convinced that the annual turnover in the chambers is good for us as well as for them."

When Rehnquist first became a justice, clerks for each justice had to review all the petitions for certiorari—the requests for the Court to hear a case. In effect, each of the justice's clerks were doing the same work. Rehnquist and his fellow newcomer, Justice Lewis F. Powell Jr., did not think this made sense. They suggested the creation of a *cert pool*—short for certiorari pool—so that the petitions for certiorari could be divided up among all the justices' clerks. Three of the other justices thought this was a good idea, and the handling of the petitions for certiorari became much more efficient.

The Most Conservative Justice

Rehnquist was pleased to serve on the Court under Chief Justice Warren Burger. While working for President Richard Nixon, Rehnquist had lobbied for Burger's confirmation to chief justice in 1969. When he became a justice himself, Rehnquist was still a strong Burger supporter. His hope was that he and Chief Justice Burger would be able to undo some of the more liberal policies made under Earl Warren, who had served as chief justice before Burger.

In a 1985 interview, Rehnquist used strong language to describe the Warren Court, comparing it to a lopsided boat. "I felt that at the time I came on the Court," he said, "the boat was kind of heeling over in one direction. Interpreting my oath as I saw it, I felt that my job was, where those sort of situations arose, to kind of lean the other way." Later, Rehnquist said he wanted to make sure that the Court "called a halt to a number of the sweeping rulings that were made in the days of the Warren Court."

In Rehnquist's opinion, most of the Warren Court's "sweeping rulings" were related to the rights of criminal defendants. He said he wanted to make "the law dealing with the constitutional rights of accused criminal defendants . . . more even-handed . . . than it was when [he] came on the Court." For example, Rehnquist wanted the Court to overturn the famous Warren Court ruling in *Mapp v. Ohio* (1961). In that case, the Court decided that evidence illegally obtained from a criminal suspect cannot be used in the suspect's trial. He also hinted that he disagreed with *Miranda v. Arizona*, which was a 1966 case from the Warren Court. This decision said that before a criminal suspect can be questioned by police, the suspect must be told of his or her rights.

In his first few years on the Court, one of the major differences in opinion between Rehnquist and the other eight justices was over the Fourteenth Amendment of the U.S. Constitution. This amendment includes a section called the Equal Protection Clause, which says that states must treat each person in the same manner. It was written to ensure that people of different races are treated equally; its aim was to prevent discrimination. For example, this clause forbids an employer from hiring or firing a person solely based on his or her race.

In the early 1970s, when Rehnquist was a new justice, the Supreme Court took on new cases related to the Fourteenth Amendment. In several instances, the other eight justices ruled that the Equal Protection Clause applied not only to racial groups, but to other groups as well. These other groups included women, illegitimate children, and *resident aliens*—non-citizens living legally in the United States.

Rehnquist believed that the Equal Protection Clause should be applied only to cases of racial discrimination, with only a very few exceptions.

His views on this and other subjects did not go unnoticed. Almost from the day he was confirmed, Rehnquist was considered the most conservative justice on the Court. *Newsweek* magazine ran an article about him titled "The Court's Mr. Right." The *New York Times* called him "the Court's most predictable conservative member." There were three other justices who had been appointed by Republican presidents, but Rehnquist

During his 14 years as an associate justice, Rehnquist held the record for most dissents by an associate justice (Getty Images)

often disagreed with these justices. In many cases, he was the only dissenter. After a few years on the Court, his clerks started calling him "the Lone Dissenter." To symbolize this, they jokingly gave him a Lone Ranger doll.

Rehnquist spent a total of 14 years as an associate justice. During that time he dissented 54 times. This set a Court record for the most dissents by an associate justice.

Affirmative Action

Racial discrimination was a major issue during the 1970s, and the Burger Court made several decisions that changed American law and culture. In 1978, the Court heard a case about *affirmative action.* Affirmative action is a policy that attempts to give education and jobs to members of minority groups, sometimes at the expense of non-minorities. The affirmative action case that the Court heard was called *Regents of the University of California v. Bakke.* It was filed by Allan Bakke, who had twice applied to the medical school at the University of California at Davis. Bakke, who was white, argued that he was denied admission on both occasions because the university wanted to admit minority students instead. Bakke's lawyers said this was unfair because Bakke's grades and test scores were higher than the scores of any of the minority students who were admitted in the two years he applied. The case received a great deal of attention, because affirmative action was becoming a "hot" issue in the United States in the late 1970s.

Justice Thurgood Marshall described the case by saying that Bakke's attorneys "are arguing about keeping somebody out and the other side is arguing about getting somebody in." In the end, the Court issued two decisions. In the first decision, which Rehnquist supported, the Court decided that the university's admission program was flawed and that Bakke should be admitted. The second decision, which Rehnquist did not support, said that it was constitutional for colleges and universities to consider an applicant's race when deciding whether to admit him or her.

The fact that the Court made two decisions on *Bakke* shows just how conflicted the Burger Court was. Some of its decisions were conservative, and some were more liberal. In several instances, such as in *Bakke,* the decisions were both. As a result, Rehnquist could not achieve his goal of moving the Court toward more conservative positions. He would have to wait another 25 years before the Court heard another case about affirmative action in universities.

Roe v. Wade

In October 1972, the Court heard one of the most controversial cases in history. In *Roe v. Wade,* a Texas woman named Jane Roe wanted to end her pregnancy by having an abortion. But in Texas, abortions were legal only if the mother's life was threatened by the pregnancy. Roe's life was not threatened, so the Court had to decide if a woman has a constitutional right to end her pregnancy. As usual, after the two sides made their arguments, the justices had a conference. During this meeting, Justice Byron White said, "I'm not going to second guess state legislatures in striking the balance in favor of abortion laws." In other words, he believed that the states should make their own laws about abortion; the Supreme Court should not tell the states what to do. Rehnquist made his position clear. "I agree with Byron," he said.

But Rehnquist and White were outnumbered. In January 1973, the Court released its decision. A majority of justices ruled that abortion was constitutional because the Fourteenth Amendment protects a person's right to privacy. In their majority opinion, the justices wrote that a state can limit this right to privacy only when there is a "compelling state interest." According to the majority, there were two "compelling interests"—reasons—that would allow the state to prevent an abortion. The first is if having an abortion would threaten the mother's health. The second is if the fetus inside the woman's body was mature enough to survive outside of the mother's body. This maturity occurs only in the last trimester—the last three months—of a woman's pregnancy.

Rehnquist did not agree with the majority's ruling. He crafted a strongly worded dissent. In it, he wrote, "To reach its result, the Court necessarily has had to find . . . a right that was apparently completely unknown to the drafters of the Amendment." He did not think *Roe v. Wade* should be decided based on the concept of "compelling state interest" because different people have different opinions about what is "compelling." As a result,

Rehnquist argued, the Court's decision required justices to use their personal values and beliefs to decide what a "compelling state interest" would be. Rehnquist had always believed that judges should not make rulings based on their own personal values. Instead, the elected representatives of a state government should make the decision. Rehnquist wrote that the complicated decision about whether to allow abortion was "more appropriate to a legislative judgment than to a judicial one."

From Minority to Majority

Later in 1973, Rehnquist and the other justices were faced with a desegregation case, *Keyes v. School District No. 1, Denver, Colorado.* In this case, the Denver School District was accused of segregating African-American students from white students. The Court ruled that busing was a valid means of desegregating the Denver School District. In its ruling, the majority said that its decision was influenced by the earlier landmark case *Brown v. Board of Education.* Rehnquist took a very different approach. He did not think there was evidence that the Denver School District was trying to create two separate schooling environments (one for whites and another for minorities). He also believed that busing, or *forced desegregation*, was not covered in *Brown v. Board of Education.* His fellow justices disagreed, and once again Rehnquist was the only dissenter.

Rehnquist's dissents were typically very well written, and his fellow justices paid close attention to them. In a *Time* magazine article, he was called "the most self-consciously literate opinion writer" on the Court. By 1975, just three years after joining the Court, his influence was being felt in the Court's decisions. This influence can be seen in the 1976 decision for *National League of Cities v. Usery*. This case asked the Court to decide if state government employees had to be paid according to the federal minimum wage. Five of the nine justices agreed with Rehnquist that states should have the freedom to set their own rules for paying their state government employees. The justices who agreed with Rehnquist were probably swayed by his earlier written opinions, in which he had made similar arguments.

In the early 1980s, the Court grew more conservative. In 1981, President Ronald Reagan appointed Sandra Day O'Connor as an associate justice. In addition to being the Court's first female justice, O'Connor was known as someone with moderate-to-conservative views. She often voted with Rehnquist and Burger. These three justices were often joined in their decisions by two moderates: Powell and White. As a result, by 1984 Rehnquist found himself in the majority in more than half of the Court's 28 cases. His law clerks in the early 1970s had called him "the Lone Dissenter," but in the mid-1980s his law clerks called him "The Boss."

In just a few years, Rehnquist and the other conservative justices had made decisions that reduced the rights of accused criminals, cut back on civil liberties, and curbed the authority of the federal government. One example of this was *Wainwright v. Witt* in 1985. This case dealt with the death penalty. Rehnquist wrote the majority opinion, in which seven out of the nine justices said prosecutors seeking the death penalty should be able to weed out jurors who oppose the death penalty. Rehnquist was also in the majority for *New Jersey v. T.L.O.*, which said that school officials did not need search warrants to search students.

By the mid-1980s, more and more critics were calling Rehnquist a Republican partisan, meaning that he strongly supported the Republican Party and its philosophy. In an interview, Rehnquist responded to this charge:

> I have written opinions and joined opinions that have said that the Fourth Amendment [which guarantees the right to freedom from unlawful searches and seizures] should be construed [in a particular] way. I've written opinions and joined opinions that say the establishment clause of the Constitution [guaranteeing freedom of speech, press, religion] should be construed in [a particular] way. Now, I've thought those things through. I think these opinions are right.

And I want to see that version of the law applied when the case comes up. If that makes me a partisan, certainly I'm a partisan. But I don't think that distinguishes me from most of my colleagues.

Many of Rehnquist's critics were professors and other scholars at law schools and universities. They charged that many of his dissents were shaped by his personal values and his personal interpretation of the Constitution. For this reason, these critics said that it was "disingenuous"—not entirely straightforward—of him to complain about liberal justices who inject their own values and viewpoints into their opinions. Rehnquist responded to this by implying that most of his critics in academia were liberal, so they were more likely to criticize a conservative like himself. In Rehnquist's view, these faculty members would probably have a bias against his legal ideas. "I do think that the political carries over some to the judicial philosophy," he said.

Keeping "Anchors to the Outside World"

Over the course of his fourteen years as an associate justice, Rehnquist's feelings about the Court evolved. In a 1985 interview, he said that when he first arrived at the Court, he had the feeling that many of the cases the justices heard were "very critical jurisprudential battles."

This sense of importance affected him. "I would get very kind of blue if I was in the minority a good deal, and feel very pleased if I was in the majority." Over time, that changed. In 1985 he said, "I think I tend to view the process now as more of an institutional one, that there probably are things to be said on both sides of issues that perhaps I didn't always think were there."

As an associate justice, Rehnquist thought it was important to get out of the Court building as much as possible. "You just have to keep anchors to the outside world," he said in 1985, "because a justice of this Court could do all of the work he has to do . . . without ever having to leave this building. The chambers are here, the courtroom is here, the library is here, the cafeteria is here. There's a gym and an exercise room." In short, almost everything he needed was in one building. But Rehnquist did not like the idea of spending all his time in this "two-dimensional world." So he made speeches at law schools around the country. He also visited law school classes and spoke with students, and he made speeches to other legal professionals. He took a painting class, which he said he liked because, "I mix with lots of people who are totally different from the kind of people I mix with regularly."

Rehnquist also found ways to add a little fun to the Court chambers. Occasionally, he exchanged notes with his clerks during Court hearings and conferences. These notes had nothing to do with the law; instead, they were trivia questions. After deciding on the answer, Rehnquist sometimes passed the note to Justice Harry Blackmun to see if he knew the answer too.

Rehnquist became known for playing practical jokes on other justices. On April Fool's Day in 1985, he put a life-size cardboard photograph of Chief Justice Burger on a sidewalk in Washington, D.C. Next to the cutout was a sign saying "Have your picture taken with the chief justice, $1." Then Rehnquist called Chief Justice Burger and asked for a ride to work. As their car passed the cut-out, Rehnquist saw the look on the chief justice's face and laughed.

Sometimes his practical jokes were related to the law. In 1983, he asked the liberal Justice Thurgood Marshall to help him play a joke on the other justices. Marshall agreed, and Rehnquist sent out an article he had written that was very critical of one of Marshall's famous opinions. Marshall pretended to be upset, and the rest of the Court staff members were convinced. Chief Justice Burger and Justice Blackmun were angry that Rehnquist was going to publish his article. They told their clerks they were going to try to stop him. Rehnquist figured that the joke had gone on long enough, so he sent out a memo saying he was not going to publish the article after all. He said he was changing his mind in honor of a Swedish holiday that required Swedes to do something nice for someone else. As a Swedish American, Rehnquist said he wanted to observe the holiday. Soon everyone knew that Rehnquist had played another practical joke on them.

In 1985, Rehnquist agreed to a major interview with the *New York Times*. This was unusual, because he rarely gave interviews. He did not want to talk about his personal life. When the interviewer asked which judges he played poker with, Rehnquist replied, "I'm not going to write your story for you." But later in the interview, the 60-year-old associate justice opened up a bit. He said that he appreciated the stability of the Court more than he had when he joined at the age of 47. "At age 60, the life tenure looks good," he said. "And I know that if I were a senior partner in a law firm, with a nice corner office and views out both windows, a bunch of young people would be walking by wondering when I was going to go on semiretired status so they could have the office."

Looking to his future, Rehnquist said that he would be interested in getting a new job when he turned 65. "But those things don't come along very often," he said. "I don't have any very good prospects except for staying here until I retire, and then probably doing a little judging, and a little teaching, or something like that."

Rehnquist probably had no idea that his future would be quite different from the one he described. The Court was about to change, and Rehnquist was not going to be retiring anytime soon.

Later that year, Chief Justice Warren Burger announced that he was retiring. This meant that President Ronald Reagan would have to appoint a new chief justice from the justices currently serving on the Court. Naturally, the Republican president wanted to nominate someone who shared his conservative views. After a short period of weighing his options, President Reagan chose William H. Rehnquist. If all went well with his confirmation, the justice now called "The Boss" by his clerks would become "the boss" of the Supreme Court.

ANOTHER CONFIRMATION HEARING

Rehnquist's nomination to chief justice immediately caused conflict. Many of the charges made against him during his 1971 confirmation battle were repeated.

Old Issues Revisited

Almost immediately after his nomination was announced, the press began to take another look at "A Random Thought on the Segregation Cases," which Rehnquist had written in 1952, during his days as a law clerk. This memo was known in the press as the "*Brown* memo" because it addressed the case *Brown v. Board of Education* and supported *Plessy v. Ferguson*, the case responsible for the "separate but equal" ruling.

When Rehnquist was questioned about the memo during his 1971 confirmation hearings, he said it did not reflect his own views. Instead, he said, the memo reflected the views of his boss, Justice Robert H. Jackson. Rehnquist repeated this explanation in his 1986 chief justice confirmation hearings. He said that he did not agree with *Plessy* and the "separate but equal" law.

Unfortunately, not everyone believed him. The Republicans on the Senate judiciary committee could see that the questions about the *Brown* memo would not go away. Some of these senators came to Rehnquist's defense. Republican Senator Orrin Hatch was one of the nominee's most vocal supporters. He complained that the memo was 35 years old, and he did not understand why the committee was discussing "ancient events as though they are important today."

Senator Hatch reminded the judiciary committee of the letter that Donald Cronson sent back in 1971, saying that he and Rehnquist had written the *Brown* memo in support of *Plessy* at the request of Justice Jackson. Senator Hatch said that Cronson's letter proved that the memo was not a reflection of Rehnquist's personal views.

But some of the Democratic senators did not think that Cronson's letter was convincing enough. Senator Edward Kennedy asked why Rehnquist had never told the Senate in 1971 that he had co-written the *Brown* memo with Cronson.

Rehnquist (right) and his wife, Natalie, at his 1986 chief justice Senate confirmation hearing (Getty Images)

Democratic Senator Howard Metzenbaum also challenged Rehnquist's credibility. He pointed to other memos the nominee had written when he was a law clerk. One of these memos included the sentence, "It is about time the Court faced the fact that the white people [in] the South don't like the colored people."

Senator Metzenbaum referred to this sentence when he questioned Rehnquist at the hearings. "Did you," Metzenbaum said, "in all of the time you worked with Justice Jackson, ever hear him say something like the following: It is about time that the Court faced the fact that the white people of the South do not like the colored people?"

"I simply cannot recall at this time," Rehnquist answered.

In asking this question, Senator Metzenbaum was trying to show that Rehnquist usually wrote memos that reflected his own opinions—not the opinions of his boss Justice Jackson.

Democratic Senator Edward Kennedy said that he thought the *Brown* memo had, in fact, reflected Rehnquist's pro-segregation views. As evidence, Senator Kennedy showed a study done by a journalist named Richard Kluger. Kluger had analyzed the *Brown* memo and compared the legal writings of Rehnquist and Justice Jackson. In his analysis, Kluger wrote that the evidence showed that "the memorandum in question—the one that threatened to deprive William Rehnquist of his place on the Supreme Court—was an accurate statement of his own views on segregation, not those of Robert Jackson, who, by contrast, was a staunch libertarian and humanist."

Two other memos regarding race relations were uncovered that were written by Rehnquist when he was a clerk. In one, Rehnquist discussed the case *Terry v. Adams.* In this case, an appeals court had ruled that a Texas Democratic club could deny African Americans the right to vote in their club election. Rehnquist supported this decision on legal grounds, not on ethical ones. He said that the ruling would seem "right to a lawyer, rather than a crusader."

There were more tough questions from the Democratic senators. Senator Joseph R. Biden Jr. held up a newspaper article. The article said that when Rehnquist was a law clerk in 1952, he had energetically defended *Plessy* during debates with other law clerks. Rehnquist admitted that he had engaged in these debates, but he said that at that time, he had not made a final decision about whether the Court should overrule *Plessy*.

Several other senators expressed concern that Rehnquist had participated in the 1972 Supreme Court case *Laird v. Tatum*. This case had questioned whether the Army should be allowed to conduct surveillance of citizens. Before becoming a justice, Rehnquist had worked on the case on behalf of the U.S. government. He had argued in favor of the Army while he was the assistant attorney general. Because of this, some people thought Rehnquist should *recuse* himself—sit out—from hearing the case with the rest of the Court. These critics said that because Rehnquist knew the case so well, he had already decided his judgment before the case was even presented to the Court.

More Issues Emerge

There were two new issues that emerged during the 1986 confirmation hearings. One issue was the news that

Rehnquist had been addicted to painkillers for nine years. The painkiller, called Placidyl, had been prescribed to help relieve Rehnquist's back pain. From 1976 to 1981, Rehnquist's prescription had been higher than the legal maximum dosage. Then, in 1981, Rehnquist was checked into a drug treatment program. This program apparently worked, because during the confirmation hearings, Rehnquist's doctor said the nominee had stopped using Placidyl and was no longer addicted to it.

The second new issue during the confirmation hearings was related to two homes Rehnquist had bought. One was a house in Arizona, which Rehnquist purchased in 1961. Another was a Vermont summer house he bought in 1974. It was discovered that the contracts for both of these houses stated that the houses could not be sold to people belonging to certain religious and racial groups. In particular, the houses could not be sold to blacks or Jews. Rehnquist said that he had not known about these aspects of the contracts until the press began running stories about them. Rehnquist's Republican supporters thought this entire issue was "ridiculous." His opponents said that a lawyer like Rehnquist surely would have read his contract before signing it. They said he had to have known that the contracts excluded minorities.

Soon, however, another issue distracted everyone. This issue was actually an old one from the 1971 confirmation hearings: whether Rehnquist had challenged African-American and Hispanic voters during elections in Phoenix. In 1971, Rehnquist had told the Senate that he had not challenged voters. He said he had only given advice to the people who were challenging voters. But in 1986 new witnesses came forward. One man who knew Rehnquist said that he had witnessed Rehnquist actually challenging voters in 1964. This witness claimed that voters complained about Rehnquist's behavior.

Another witness said that in 1962 and 1964, he had seen Rehnquist in meetings with other Republicans. The witness claimed that Rehnquist said they should challenge unqualified voters, including illiterates.

Yet another witness said that he had seen Rehnquist challenge an African-American man in 1964. According to the witness, Rehnquist told the man that he might not be allowed to vote. The man got mad, and this led to a "shoving match" between him and Rehnquist.

These accusations made the confirmation hearings very dramatic. The people involved were firmly divided by political party lines. Republican senators said that all the witnesses were Democrats and therefore their testimony was suspicious.

When Rehnquist was questioned about whether he had challenged voters, he said he did not "believe" that he had.

Finally, the judiciary committee decided to vote on whether to allow Rehnquist's nomination to go to the full Senate. Five members of the committee—all Democrats—voted against Rehnquist. But thirteen members voted in his favor. Now it was up to the entire Senate to decide whether William H. Rehnquist should become the chief justice.

Confirmation in the Senate

Unfortunately for Rehnquist, when his nomination moved to the Senate, some new problems emerged. A group of civil rights organizations protested his confirmation. The Women's Legal Defense Fund criticized him for opposing the Equal Rights Amendment, which gave full and equal rights to women. Rehnquist had signed a memo in 1970 that said that this amendment would lead to the "dissolution of the family." But Rehnquist's supporters said that the memo did not represent his personal opinions. Instead, it offered a list of reasons that people might oppose the amendment.

Another problem for Rehnquist was the public. A national poll found that 30 percent of Americans supported his confirmation and 58 percent did not.

But the biggest threat to Rehnquist's nomination came from his wife Nan's brother, Harold Cornell. For many years, Harold had been suffering from a disease called multiple sclerosis. In the early 1960s he was forced to retire because of his disease. Unable to work, he quickly ran out of money. In an interview with the *New York Times*, Harold said that he was forced to live off of the $96 that Social Security gave him each month. In the early 1960s, he went to a family reunion and asked his siblings if he could get money from a fund his parents had set up for emergencies before they died. In his *New York Times* interview, Harold described the meeting during the family reunion. "Bill [Rehnquist] was at that meeting," Harold said. "He certainly knew . . . that I was disabled and in serious financial straits. Bill and the others [in the family] decided I didn't have the right to the emergency trust fund even though I was 100 percent disabled." Harold also said that he had learned about a trust fund that his father had set up just for him, but which his family, including Rehnquist, never told him about.

Harold's interview was published in the midst of Rehnquist's confirmation hearing. Suddenly many people— including Harold—were accusing Rehnquist of unethical conduct. They said that Rehnquist mismanaged the trust and that for this reason he should not become chief justice.

Rehnquist did not want to speak to the media about these accusations. A Supreme Court spokesperson said that Rehnquist had a policy of not talking to the press about his confirmation. However, some of Harold's family members said that Rehnquist had not done anything wrong. They said that Harold's father wanted Rehnquist to keep the fund a secret because Harold had a reputation for wasting money. Critics wondered if this was true; why would Harold's father set up a fund for him and then not want Harold to know about it? A legal ethics scholar suggested that Rehnquist's behavior was "especially wrong" because his wife Nan benefited financially when her father's money was not being distributed to Harold.

Four Democratic senators requested that the FBI reopen an investigation into Rehnquist's past, but this was denied on the grounds that the FBI had known about this charge.

On September 11, 1986, the Senate began debating Rehnquist's nomination. The debates lasted for five days. Democrats repeated their accusations of unethical behavior and dishonesty. Republican senators fought back. They said that the Democrats' complaints were "much ado about very little." They also said that these charges were far back in the past. Most importantly, Republican supporters pointed out that there had not been any serious complaints about Rehnquist's actions or behavior as an associate justice on the Supreme Court. In the end, in a vote of 65 to 33, Rehnquist was confirmed as chief justice.

Rehnquist is sworn in as chief justice by Chief Justice Warren Burger as Mrs. Rehnquist and President Ronald Reagan look on. (Time Life Pictures/Getty Images)

Afterward, Rehnquist was asked about the debate in the Senate. He answered, "I'm not going to address myself really to the past. That's over, that chapter is closed, and I'm looking forward to the future and to trying to be a good chief justice."

7

CHIEF JUSTICE REHNQUIST

It was clear that most of the other justices on the Court were looking forward to Rehnquist moving into his new position. Whereas his predecessor, Chief Justice Burger, had seemed pompous and aggressive, Rehnquist was known to be very diplomatic. Even the liberal justices, like Thurgood Marshall, considered Rehnquist to be considerate and easy to work with. And, of course, Rehnquist was well known as a practical joker with a good sense of humor.

Getting the Office Organized

Rehnquist's transition to chief justice went fairly smoothly. Soon after being sworn in on September 26, 1986, Rehnquist moved from his old one-room office to the chief justice's office. This office has two rooms that are separated by the Court's conference room. The two rooms are rather small, but Rehnquist does not mind. "I have never thought," he once wrote, "that just because one held an important position it was necessary to have an office the size of the one Italian dictator Benito Mussolini had, and so I have no complaint about the change. In my present location I am much closer to the conference room and to the courtroom than I was in my old location." For Rehnquist, there is another bonus to being so close to these places. "As a result, I have been more punctual for sessions of the Court and the conference than I was in the past."

Since becoming chief justice, Rehnquist has had two secretaries and an aide. The secretaries answer the telephone and collect and organize the letters that Rehnquist receives and sends. They also type what he dictates to them. Among other tasks, his aide makes and circulates photocopies and helps prepare and serve meals.

Just as important as his secretaries and his aide are his law clerks. When he became an associate justice in 1972, Rehnquist had only three law clerks each year. This number did not change when Rehnquist became chief justice. Even today, he has only three clerks—and he picks them himself. In his book *The Supreme Court,* Rehnquist wrote about how he chooses and works with his clerks:

> Having good clerks is a very important factor in the proper functioning of my chambers . . . When I was a clerk the Ivy League schools had a virtual monopoly

on the jobs, but that is no longer the case, at least in my chambers. In the spring of each year I receive several hundred applications to be a law clerk for the term of the Court commencing the summer of the next year, and I go through the applications myself in an effort to winnow them down to somewhere around fifteen. I look through each résumé for indications that the applicant has done very well in law school. I prefer that the applicant has had a responsible position on the law review, because I think law review is an excellent teaching device whereby one learns to organize, assemble, and develop one's ideas and to work with other people. Service on law review certainly does not teach one to write sparkling or even interesting prose, but it does teach one to organize and logically develop one's train of thought.

Rehnquist also wrote that he looks for "clerks who seem to have a sense of humor, and who do not give the impression of being too sold upon themselves."

Rehnquist's clerks start working in July, after the Court begins its summer recess. Their summer is spent doing what Rehnquist himself did when he clerked for Justice Jackson: reading and evaluating petitions for certiorari.

Unlike some other justices, Rehnquist does not want his clerks to write long, detailed evaluations and memos.

Instead, he likes to receive a very short memo with all of the case's main points outlined. One former clerk said that the chief justice "likes to get his work done and get home."

But perhaps the most important task for Rehnquist's clerks is the drafting of opinions. "In my case, the clerks do the first draft of almost all cases to which I have been assigned to write the Court's opinion," Rehnquist said. Occasionally, if the clerks have a lot of opinions to write, Rehnquist will write the first draft of an opinion himself, but this is uncommon. Typically, Rehnquist tells his clerks how he wants the opinion to be written, but he allows them a good amount of flexibility.

Rehnquist is not the only justice to have his clerks write the first drafts of opinions. Most of the other justices follow the same procedure. "I think the practice is entirely proper," Rehnquist said. "The justice must retain for himself control not merely of the outcome of the case, but of the explanation of the outcome, and I do not believe this practice sacrifices either." In some instances, Rehnquist said, he might rewrite the clerk's entire draft. Or, he said, "I may leave it relatively unchanged." Ultimately, he said, "the individual justices still continue to do a great deal more of their own work than do their counterparts in other branches of the federal government."

Decisions, Decisions

Shortly before becoming chief justice, Rehnquist described the attributes he thinks a Supreme Court justice must have. "I think you have to be interested in the law, as a kind of discipline," he said. "I think you can be a successful lawyer without having any great interest in the law. I'm not sure that you could be a successful . . . judge without having an interest in the law. I think you also have to enjoy writing. And you have to enjoy analyzing things." More importantly, he said, "you have to be able to stand on your own two feet. [You can't be] bamboozled by currents, trendy ideas, that sort of thing . . . Not easily conned. Not awash in current trends of public opinion."

He also explained how he saw the role of the Supreme Court. Not surprisingly, he said that the Court should not use judicial activism to push an agenda, that is, judges should not allow their personal feelings reflect on their decisions. "I don't know that a Court should really have a sense of mission," he said in 1985. "I think the sense of mission comes from the president or the House of Representatives or the Senate. They're supposed to be the motive force in our government. The Supreme Court and the federal judiciary are more the brakes that say, 'You're trying to do this, but you can't do it that way.'" In other words, Rehnquist saw the Court as an institution that can analyze legislation introduced by elected officials. "The idea that the Court should be way out in front saying, 'Look, this is the way the country ought to go,' I don't think that was ever the purpose of the Court."

Although his critics have sometimes called him a Republican partisan, Rehnquist has said that he thinks the Court should include a range of judicial perspectives. It would be dangerous, he said, for all the justices to have the exact same views as the chief justice. "Anything like a one-man or, I suppose in this day, a one-person Supreme Court would be an incredibly tyrannical thing." So although he wouldn't want all the other justices to think just like him, he said, "I would welcome two or three!"

In Rehnquist's first year as chief justice, the Court seemed evenly split between conservatives, moderates, and liberals. The following year, however, Justice Powell retired, and President Reagan was able to appoint Anthony Kennedy. Thus, by 1987 the Rehnquist Court had five conservative justices: Rehnquist, Kennedy, O'Connor, White, and Antonin Scalia.

Occasionally, however, these conservative justices did not agree, so the five-person majority did not always hold together. In fact, Rehnquist sometimes surprised people by making decisions that went against conservative or Republican views. For example, in *Morrison v. Olson* (1987), he disagreed with President Reagan over whether

Congress can appoint independent counsels—investigators—to investigate government officials.

In other cases, all nine of the justices agreed and the Court issued a unanimous ruling. Rehnquist once said his role model was Charles Evans Hughes, who was chief justice from 1930 to 1941. Rehnquist praised Hughes's belief that unanimous rulings made the public more confident in the Court. He also admired how Hughes modified "his own opinions to hold or increase his majority." Rehnquist's own actions as a chief justice made it clear that he was following Hughes's example. In the 1987 term, Rehnquist agreed with the liberal Justice Thurgood Marshall in 57.6 percent of cases. (He agreed with Justice Kennedy, a conservative, in 83.1 percent of cases.) By the end of that term, Rehnquist's fellow justices were praising his work. He had reduced the number of cases the Court took on, which helped them accomplish the rare feat of finishing their term before July 1. After all these successes, Justice Blackmun called Rehnquist a "splendid administrator in conference."

Like other chief justices, Rehnquist has worked hard to make sure that the Court keeps its actions confidential. There has not been a photograph of the Court in session since 1935. Television cameras have never been allowed in the Court, and neither has a radio microphone. Clerks have to follow a Code of Conduct that forbids them from talking publicly about the Court's work, even among friends and family. One reason for this is that the justices do not want to have to worry that the public will find out about their thought processes when they're weighing the facts of the case. One justice, Hugo Black, was so concerned about privacy that he had his family burn all of his conference notes before he died.

Criminal Procedures

Rehnquist's conservative philosophy can be seen in his rulings on criminal procedures. In a series of decisions, the Rehnquist Court has strengthened victims' rights and weakened criminals' rights. In 1991, it had several notable victories. In *Harmelin v. Michigan*, Rehnquist led a majority that upheld a life sentence without parole for a first-time drug offender. In *Arizona v. Fulminante,* the Court ruled that *coerced*—forced—confessions at a trial did not mean that a conviction should automatically be overturned. Until this ruling, convicted criminals could have their sentences overturned if they could prove that the police had coerced them into making a confession. Under Rehnquist's majority ruling, a conviction could stand if it could be proven that the defendant would have been convicted even without the coerced confession.

For Rehnquist, however, the biggest victory may have been in 1991's *Payne v. Tennessee*. This case gave him another chance to look at victim impact statements. These statements are used when a court is trying to decide how to punish someone convicted of murder. They allow a victim's relative to make a statement to the court explaining how the victim's death has affected the family and community. Rehnquist supported the use of victim impact statements. But in 1987 the Court made it illegal for prosecutors to use the statements. Ever since that time, Rehnquist had wanted to find another case that would allow the court to reconsider these statements.

Payne v. Tennessee was the perfect case for this. Pervis Payne had been convicted for murdering a mother and her daughter. At Payne's sentencing, the prosecutor called the victim's relatives to the stand to talk about how the murders affected the family. Payne wanted to have his death sentence reconsidered. He said that the Supreme Court's 1987 ruling made it illegal for victims' relatives to make impact statements. So Payne sued the state of Tennessee.

The liberal justices on the Court did not want to consider this case. They felt that the issue of victim impact statements had been settled four years before, and did not need to be revisited. Justice John Paul Stevens said it was "unnecessary and unwise" to take on the case. But Rehnquist felt very strongly. In February 1991, he convinced Justices O'Connor, Scalia, and Kennedy to vote to hear the case. As chief justice, he was able to put the case on the fast track. Normally, a case granted in February would not be heard until October or November. But Rehnquist arranged for the case to be heard by the end of the Court's spring session. It was a fast and sweet victory for Rehnquist, who wrote the majority opinion.

That year was a high point for Rehnquist professionally. But 1991 also brought him personal tragedy. In October his wife of 38 years, Nan, died. Rehnquist, now age 67, became a widower, and he has remained single ever since.

Abortion

Three years after becoming chief justice, Rehnquist and his fellow justices confronted the very controversial issue of abortion. Since *Roe v. Wade* in 1973, which ruled that abortion was legal, Rehnquist had been hoping to revisit the issue of abortion and overturn *Roe*. In 1989, the case *Webster v. Reproductive Services* offered him and other *Roe* opponents an opportunity to do just that.

The case was a challenge to a Missouri law that made it illegal for public employees and public health facilities to provide abortions or to give counseling about abortion. The only exception to this law was if the pregnancy put the mother in a "life-threatening" situation. The law also said that human life begins at conception.

Even before the case was argued in Court, Rehnquist probably had a good idea of how the justices would vote. Justices Rehnquist, Scalia, and White were known for wanting to reverse *Roe v. Wade* and make abortion illegal. Justices Blackmun, Brennan, Marshall, and Stevens were known for supporting *Roe*. That left Justices O'Connor and Kennedy, both of whom were on record as supporting the right to abortion in some cases. It was easy for anyone to see that Rehnquist, Scalia, and White would be outnumbered. The only way the Court would completely overturn *Roe* was if the other justices decided that life begins at conception. But this seemed very unlikely.

In the end, the Court did not make a ruling on whether life begins at conception. It did not completely overturn *Roe v. Wade*. A majority of justices, however, did say that it was legal for Missouri to prohibit abortions in public facilities unless the mother's life was endangered by the pregnancy. This was a small but important victory for Rehnquist and the other conservatives.

Since that ruling, the Rehnquist court has made other decisions on abortion. Some decisions have put more limits on abortion rights. For example, *Hodgson v. Minnesota* (1990) upheld Minnesota's law that a female under the age of 18 must notify at least one parent that she is considering getting an abortion. After this notification, the female must wait 48 hours before having the abortion. Rehnquist was in the majority in this opinion.

Other rulings have prevented states from limiting abortion rights. In *Stenberg v. Carhart* (2000), the Court ruled on the issue of "partial birth" abortions, in which the fetus is so developed that it requires a special procedure to be aborted. The Court decided that the ban was too vague and could be interpreted as a ban against all abortions. Rehnquist was in the minority in this opinion.

Affirmative Action

As an associate justice, Rehnquist had been frustrated by the Burger Court's support of affirmative action. He had wanted to move the Court in a more conservative direction. He did not believe that affirmative action was fair.

During Rehnquist's time as chief justice, the Court has had several opportunities to address affirmative action in the work place. Until 2003, however, the Court did not have a chance to look at affirmative action in higher education. That year, the Court heard two cases about using race as a factor in higher education admissions. In the first case, *Gratz v. Bollinger*, the Court had to decide if the undergraduate admissions policy at University of Michigan was legal. This policy used a point system to evaluate an applicant. It gave minority applicants 20 extra points. Opponents of the policy said that this was unfair. They said that since the point system had a maximum of 100 points, minority students were getting an unfair advantage simply for being members of a minority.

As Rehnquist and the other justices heard the arguments in court, many people were paying close attention. Most observers assumed that the five more conservative justices would reach a majority and rule against the policy. They also assumed that the four more liberal justices would rule in favor of the policy. So when the ruling was announced, some were surprised by the results. Justice Stephen Breyer, usually considered a liberal, joined Rehnquist and four other justices in condemning the point policy. In the 6–3 decision, the Court said that the point system was unfair and needed to be replaced. The majority opinion suggested that state universities like University of Michigan should hire more employees to read all the applications and judge each one individually. That way, they would not need to use the point policy.

But the Court also had to consider another, even more important affirmative action case. In *Grutter v. Bollinger,* the Court had to decide whether University of Michigan's law school could explicitly favor admitting minority students. The case was filed by Barbara Grutter, a white student who applied to the law school and was rejected. When she learned that some minority students with lower test scores were admitted, she said the university was discriminating against her for being white.

Many people expected the Court to rule against the university once again. When the ruling was announced, however, once again many people were surprised. This time, the surprise came from Justice O'Connor. Although she often voted with Rehnquist and the other conservatives, in this case she joined four of the more liberal justices in upholding University of Michigan's policy. In a 5–4 ruling, the Court said that the use of race in admissions was acceptable because the university was trying to attain a "critical mass"—a solid presence—of a diverse student body, including minorities.

This law school decision was much more important than the one regarding the use of points. That is because the law

Chief Justice Rehnquist is sworn in to preside over the impeachment trial of President Clinton. (Associated Press, U.S. Senate)

school decision was more general; it ruled that affirmative action is legal. It said that a college or university could explicitly try to attract and accept more minority students. The point policy case, on the other hand, said that the *specific* way the University of Michigan was trying to attain diversity—through a point system—had to change. The university could still aim for a diverse student body, but it had to find another admissions system to do so.

After two such high-profile cases, it is very unlikely that the Court will consider another affirmative action case.

President Clinton's Impeachment Trial

In 1998, Chief Justice Rehnquist had to perform a duty that only two other chief justices had ever performed. He had to preside over a trial of a U.S. president.

Earlier in the year, President Bill Clinton had been accused of having an affair with a woman who worked in the White House. At first the president denied the charges. Later, he admitted them. The House of Representatives voted to *impeach* the president—formally accuse him of wrongdoing and try him in court. The impeachment trial would determine whether the president would be removed from office. The next step was for the Senate to hold a trial. According to the law, the judge at a Senate trial has to be the chief justice of the Supreme Court.

The trial began in January 1999. Suddenly, Rehnquist was in the public eye again. He had not received so much attention since his confirmation hearings. The press examined everything he did. Newspapers showed pictures of Rehnquist's special judge's robe, which he had personally designed. The robe had four gold stripes on each sleeve. It was modeled after a costume he had seen in a stage production of a famous musical.

But there were far more serious issues than the chief justice's robe. The impeachment trial deeply divided the American public. The senators who were trying to impeach the president believed that Clinton had lied under oath. In doing so, they said, he had damaged the reputation of the U.S. presidency. Some of the president's supporters, on the other hand, said that he had not lied under oath. Other supporters argued that even if he was guilty, the lie he told was about a personal affair, not a matter of government.

Throughout the trial, Rehnquist was quite strict. Once, the Senate's majority leader asked if his fellow senators could have a short break. The chief justice said they could not.

However, Rehnquist also displayed his famous wit. He frequently made jokes to the senators. He made them laugh when he talked about how much livelier the Senate is compared to the Supreme Court. He said, "I underwent the sort of culture shock that naturally occurs when one moves from the very structured environment of the Supreme Court to what I shall call . . . the more free-form environment of the Senate."

On February 12, the Senate voted not to remove President Clinton from office. With the verdict in, Rehnquist told the senators that they had impressed him. "I leave you now a wiser, but not a sadder man," he said. "I have been impressed by the manner in which the majority leader [a Republican] and the minority leader [a Democrat] have agreed on procedural rules in spite of the differences that separate their two parties on matters of substance." He went on to say that he was impressed by "the quality of debate" that the senators had engaged in.

By the end of the trial, most Americans felt that the political system worked. And, for the first time, many of them could put a face to the name of the chief justice of the United States.

8

BUSH V. GORE

Of all the decisions in the Rehnquist Court, *Bush v. Gore* was by far the most controversial. This decision, made in 2000, determined who became the president of the United States. For Rehnquist, it was an extremely stressful experience. It has also become the most criticized decision his Court had ever made. To understand how *Bush v. Gore* ended up in the Supreme Court, it is first necessary to understand how an American president is usually elected.

Too Close to Call

Every four years there is a presidential election in the United States. The system that is used to elect a president in the U.S. is called the Electoral College. In this system, the candidate who gets the most votes across the country is not always the winner of the presidential election. Instead, the candidate who has the most *electoral votes* in each state is the winner. The number of electoral votes in a state is determined by adding the state's number of senators and congresspeople. For example, South Dakota has three electoral votes because it has two senators and one congressperson. California, however, has 54 electoral votes because it has two senators and 52 congresspeople. Whichever candidate has the highest number of *popular—direct—*votes in each state gets all of that state's electoral votes. Because each state has a different number of electoral votes, it is possible for a candidate to win the majority of popular votes but still not win the Electoral College.

This is what happened in the 2000 election between George W. Bush and Al Gore. On November 7, 2000, over 100 million Americans voted. Early results that day showed that Al Gore had the majority of popular votes, and a slim majority of electoral votes. But the votes in Florida still had not been counted. Whichever candidate won Florida's 25 electoral votes would become president.

The race was very close. By the end of the day, it still was not clear which candidate had the most votes. The next morning, initial results showed 6 million Floridians had voted, and that Bush had 1,800 more popular votes than Gore. Under Florida law, the election board had to recount the votes by machine because Bush's lead was so narrow.

At the same time, many people were complaining that they had not been able to vote. They said that they had turned up at the voting booths and been told, incorrectly, that they were not registered to vote. Many of these people were Democrats, who probably would have voted for Gore. The mood in the country was becoming very tense.

The Florida election board began to recount the votes by machine. Gore, however, said that this method did not work. He and his supporters said that the machines could not correctly read the paper ballots. He asked the Florida courts to allow election officials to recount the ballots by hand. Bush opposed this. He felt it was fairer to have machines read the ballots rather than humans, who would

The 2000 presidential election was hotly contested by both the public and the candidates. The Supreme Court eventually had to make a decision in the case. (Associated Press)

have to use their judgment—and their personal opinions—to decide how to read some ballots. He wanted the recounts to stop. In his view, the machine recount had determined that he was the winner.

By now, the entire world was watching Florida, waiting to see who would become the next president. Supporters for Bush and Gore began arguing and, in some cases, fighting.

The Courts Get Involved

On November 13, 2000, a federal judge in Florida ruled against Bush. He said the recounts could continue. On November 15, the Florida Supreme Court ruled that the deadline for finishing the hand recounts could be extended by 12 days.

But voting officials in some parts of Florida said that even with the additional 12 days, they would not be able to finish counting the ballots by hand. Because of this, they stopped counting. Other areas of Florida continued counting. On November 26, the Florida Secretary of State ruled that she could not accept the recount numbers because they were submitted two hours past the deadline. She declared that Bush was the winner.

Gore decided to fight this decision. The Florida Supreme Court listened to his argument and ordered a hand recount of certain ballots. Bush appealed this decision to the U.S. Supreme Court.

Rehnquist and the other justices had to decide whether to accept the case. They knew that the world was watching, and that Americans were getting very impatient. The public wanted the crisis to be over. The justices met privately, without even their law clerks present. Because there is no public record of these discussions, only the justices know what was talked about in that meeting. We do know, however, that the Court eventually accepted the case.

On December 11, 2000, the Bush and Gore lawyers presented their arguments to the Court. Normally, a decision on a Court case is not released until many weeks or months after the case is presented to the Court. But Rehnquist and the other justices knew that the Court had to act very quickly. After listening to the arguments from both sides, the justices met in secret and discussed the case. Rehnquist and Kennedy were very concerned that different areas of Florida were counting their ballots in different ways. Justices Breyer and Souter suggested that the Court ask Florida to establish a standard ballot-counting method that would offer equal protection. That way, all areas would be counting the ballots in the same way. But not everyone agreed with this idea.

Late the next night, Rehnquist led a 5–4 majority that ruled that the recounts should not continue. All of the justices in the majority agreed that they could not ask Florida to do a more thorough recount because it was already December 12, which was the legal deadline for determining who won Florida's electoral votes. There were other reasons as well. In the majority opinion, Rehnquist wrote that when the Florida Supreme Court asked for more recounts, it was trying to take power away from Florida's state legislature. A longtime advocate of states' rights, Rehnquist believed that the legislature, not the Florida Supreme Court, should have the final say.

Justices Scalia and Thomas said that they would add their names to Rehnquist's opinion, but Justices Kennedy and O'Connor refused to do so. Instead, they wanted to write their own opinion. Their reason for voting with the majority was that they believed that the different methods of counting votes were unconstitutional because they did not give "equal protection" to all the voters. Also, O'Connor wanted to make sure the majority opinion said that the ruling should be "limited to the present circumstances." In other words, she did not want the ruling to be used as an example in future elections.

Rehnquist seemed to think that it was important for the majority to be united. So, rather than release two majority opinions, Rehnquist, Scalia, and Thomas signed their names to the opinion written by O'Connor and Kennedy.

The justices left the Court building late that night. They were obviously tired. The *New York Times* said that Justices

Chief Justice Rehnquist has decided many landmark cases during his time on the Supreme Court. (Landov)

Scalia and Breyer looked "grim but determined" as they drove away from the building, and that Justice Souter looked "hollow-eyed and ashen."

In addition to being tired, the four dissenting justices were clearly angry. In his dissent, Justice Stevens wrote with surprising bitterness that the decision "can only lend credence to the most cynical appraisal of the work of judges throughout the land." He also wrote, "Although we may never know with complete certainty the identity of the winner of this year's presidential election, the identity of the loser is perfectly clear. It is the nation's confidence in the judge as an impartial guardian of the rule of law."

Many Americans agreed. Gore's supporters claimed that the Supreme Court had "awarded" the presidency to Bush. Some people said that Bush had not been elected. Instead, they said, Bush had been "selected" by the Court. Some newspaper editorials said that the Court had damaged its reputation by getting involved in the case and stopping the recount.

But other people supported the Court's decision. These people said that the Court had to step in so that the country could settle on a president.

Since the 2000 decision in _Bush v. Gore,_ Rehnquist and the other justices have said very little about _Bush v. Gore._ It seems that by remaining silent, the Court has been trying to heal the wounds of this landmark case.

THE REHNQUIST COURT IN THE NEW MILLENNIUM

In the new millennium, Rehnquist has made some predictable and some surprising votes. Few people were surprised when, in 2003, he voted against affirmative action in university admissions. Nor was it surprising when he voted in favor of long sentences for nonviolent crimes, or when he voted against overturning laws against homosexual activity in Texas. All of these rulings were in keeping with his lifelong judicial beliefs. However, in recent years Rehnquist has disagreed with some of the opinions of the other conservative justices—especially

Scalia and Thomas. For example, in 2003 Rehnquist voted that state employees can sue their state government for not letting them take time off for family emergencies. Rehnquist said that the states had to recognize the federal government's Family and Medical Leave Act. For someone who often advocates states' rights, this decision was a bit surprising. In the majority opinion, Rehnquist wrote that the Family and Medical Leave Act is important because it helps fight stereotypes about mothers who work. He said the law helped "dismantle persisting gender-based barriers" facing women in the workplace.

Another decision that surprised some legal experts was *Locke v. Davey* (2004). In this case, the Court was asked to consider whether the state of Washington must provide scholarships to students seeking training to become Christian ministers. Washington provides scholarships for other areas of study, but it said that it cannot provide scholarships for religious training because its constitution forbids using public money to support a specific religion. This case was fairly similar to a 2002 case, in which Rehnquist and the other conservative justices had ruled that public funds could be used to send children to parochial, or religious, schools. Because of this decision in 2002, some legal experts thought Rehnquist would rule against the state of Washington. But in the end, the decision was 7–2 in favor of Washington's policy. Rehnquist wrote the majority opinion. His two most conservative colleagues, Justices Scalia and Thomas, were the only dissenters.

Because of decisions like this one, Rehnquist is no longer considered the Court's most conservative member. In the 2003 term, he was right behind Justice O'Connor in having the fewest dissents. This is a far cry from his voting record as the "Lone Dissenter" in the early 1970s. Back then, he dissented more often than any other justice—and often he was the only dissenter.

When Rehnquist was confirmed as chief justice in 1986, many liberals were worried that he would move the Court in a conservative direction. Although he certainly has made many conservative decisions, the current Court is less rigidly conservative than many had predicted.

What's Next?

Rehnquist has described himself as a history buff. He has written four books about politics and law. In 1987 he published *The Supreme Court: How It Was, How It Is*. This book is a history of the Supreme Court that presents famous decisions within their historical context. In 1992 he published *Grand Inquests: The Historical Impeachments of Justice Samuel Chase and President Andrew Johnson*. This book chronicles two of the country's most famous impeachment cases. In 2000, he published *All the Laws but One: Civil Liberties in Wartime*. In 2004, he published a

Supreme Court Justices Sandra Day O'Connor (left) and Anthony Kennedy (right) join Chief Justice Rehnquist (center) in breaking ground for an expansion and modernization of the U.S. Supreme Court complex in 2003. (Landov)

book called *Centennial Crisis: The Disputed Election of 1876.* This was a particularly interesting subject for a chief justice who had been criticized—and praised—for the handling of the disputed election of 2000.

Rehnquist has discussed writing other books. One is a biography of Isaac C. Parker, a federal judge in the Western District of Arkansas. He was known as the "hanging judge" because he sentenced 164 criminals to death by hanging between 1875 and 1896. Many decades ago, when Rehnquist drove from Washington to Phoenix to begin his private legal practice, he stopped in Arkansas to do some research. "I gathered some fascinating minutiae with a view to eventually writing a biography," he said. He pored through old newspaper articles and court records to find his information. What interested him, he said, was that "Judge Parker's trials were swift, and there was no appeal, but the fundamentals of due process were undoubtedly present."

In October 2004, Rehnquist underwent surgery for thyroid cancer. The public was very concerned at the news of Rehnquist's health problems. Many wondered whether he would be able to continue with his work. In the weeks and months following his surgery, Rehnquist worked from his home in Virginia and did not appear in public. People waited to see if he would be able to appear at the presidential inauguration in 2005.

One month before the inauguration, Rehnquist announced that he would be at the event. On January 20, 2005, a visibly frail Rehnquist, walking with a cane, made his first public appearance since his surgery. On the steps of the U.S. Capitol, he administered the oath of office to George W. Bush, who was beginning his second term as president. Although Rehnquist's normally deep voice was raspy from illness, he smiled at the crowd and proceeded with his duties with the same determination that had defined his remarkable legal career.

TIME LINE

1924   Born on October 24 in Shorewood, Wisconsin

1932   Showing his dislike for Democratic president Franklin D. Roosevelt, the young Rehnquist says he wants to "change the government" when he grows up

1941   Editor of high school newspaper; after U.S. enters World War II, he enlists as a volunteer civil defense officer

1942   Begins freshman year at Kenyon College in Ohio

1943   Enlists in the pre-meteorology program with the U.S. Army Air Force; travels across the U.S. for training

1945   Is sent to Cairo, Egypt with other Air Force weather forecasters; from Cairo, he moves to Tripoli, Casablanca, and Tunis

1946   Returns to U.S. to go back to college; enrolls at Stanford University in California

1948 Graduates from Stanford with a B.A. and M.A. in political science; enrolls in M.A. program in government at Harvard University in Massachusetts

1950 Graduates from Harvard and enrolls in Stanford Law School; becomes editor of *Stanford Law Review*

1951 Is selected by Justice Robert H. Jackson for Supreme Court clerkship

1952 Moves to Washington, D.C., and begins 18-month clerkship with Justice Jackson

1953 Marries Natalie (Nan) Cornell; the newlyweds move to Phoenix, Arizona, and Rehnquist enters a private law practice

1955 Son, James, is born

1957 Daughter Janet is born; Rehnquist writes article for *U.S. News and World Report* criticizing some Supreme Court law clerks for being too liberal; becomes increasingly involved in Arizona's Republican Party

1958 Selected to serve as special state prosecutor for Arizona

1959 Daughter Nancy is born

1964   Campaigns in support of Republican presidential candidate Barry Goldwater; befriends Richard Kleindienst on the campaign

1968   Works with Kleindienst on Republican presidential campaign for Richard Nixon; after Nixon's victory, Rehnquist is named assistant attorney general for the Office of Legal Counsel in the Justice Department; moves back to Washington, D.C., with his family

1971   Nominated by President Nixon to be associate justice of the Supreme Court; after a difficult confirmation hearing, he is confirmed 68–28

1972   In first year as a Supreme Court justice, earns a reputation as a lone dissenter in cases

1973   Dissents in *Roe v. Wade*, which said that abortion was legal

1976   His influence begins to be felt on the Court; votes with the majority in *National League of Cities v. Usery*, which gives states the right to determine whether state government employees have to be paid according to federal minimum wage

1978   Dissents in an important affirmative action case, *Regents of the University of California v. Bakke*

1986 After a tough confirmation hearing, he becomes chief justice of the Supreme Court

1987 Publishes *The Supreme Court: How It Was, How It Is*, a history of the Court

1991 His wife Nan dies; Rehnquist and other conservative justices have several important victories in the area of strengthening victims' rights and weakening criminals' rights

1992 Publishes *Grand Inquests: The Historical Impeachments of Justice Samuel Chase and President Andrew Johnson*

1998 Presides over President Bill Clinton's impeachment trial

2000 Votes in the majority of *Bush v. Gore,* the Court's most controversial case; publishes *All the Laws but One: Civil Liberties in Wartime*

2003 Votes in the minority on *Grutter v. Bollinger*, which allows colleges and universities to maintain affirmative action policies in admissions

2004 Publishes *Centennial Crisis: The Disputed Election of 1876*

HOW TO
BECOME A
LAWYER OR
JUDGE

THE JOB

All lawyers may give legal advice and represent clients in
court when necessary. No matter what their specialty is,
their job is to help clients know their rights under the law
and then help them achieve these rights before a judge,
jury, government agency, or other legal forum, such as an
arbitration panel. Lawyers may represent businesses and
individuals. For businesses, they manage tax matters,
arrange for stock to be issued, handle claims cases, represent the firm in real estate dealings, and advise on all
legal matters. For individuals they may be trustees,
guardians, or executors; they may draw up wills or contracts

or advise on income taxes or on the purchase or sale of a home. Some work solely in the courts; others carry on most of their business outside of court, doing such tasks as drawing up mortgages, deeds, contracts, and other legal documents or by handling the background work necessary for court cases, which might include researching cases in a law library or interviewing witnesses. A number of lawyers work to establish and enforce laws for the federal and state governments by drafting legislation, representing the government in court, or serving as judges.

Lawyers can also take positions as professors in law schools. Administrators, research workers, and writers are also important to the profession. Administrative positions in business or government may be of a nonlegal nature, but the qualities, background, and experience of a lawyer are often helpful in such positions.

Other individuals with legal training may choose not to practice but instead opt for careers in which their background and knowledge of law are important. These careers include tax collectors, credit investigators, FBI agents, insurance adjusters, process servers, and probation officers.

Some of the specialized fields for lawyers include the following:

Civil lawyers work in a field also known as private law. They focus on damage suits and breach-of-contract suits;

prepare and draw up deeds, leases, wills, mortgages, and contracts; and act as trustees, guardians, or executors of an estate when necessary.

Criminal lawyers, also known as *defense lawyers,* specialize in cases dealing with offenses committed against society or the state, such as theft, murder, or arson. They interview clients and witnesses to ascertain facts in a case, correlate their findings with known cases, and prepare a case to defend a client against the charges made. They conduct a defense at the trial, examine witnesses, and summarize the case with a closing argument to a jury.

District attorneys, also known as *prosecuting attorneys,* represent the city, county, state, or federal government in court proceedings. They gather and analyze evidence and review legal material relevant to a lawsuit. Then they present their case to the grand jury, which decides whether the evidence is sufficient for an indictment. If it is not, the suit is dismissed and there is no trial. If the grand jury decides to indict the accused, however, the case goes to court, where the district attorney appears before the judge and jury to present evidence against the defendant.

Probate lawyers specialize in planning and settling estates. They draw up wills, deeds of trust, and similar documents for clients who want to plan for giving their belongings to their heirs when they die. Upon a client's death, probate lawyers vouch for the validity of the will and represent the executors and administrators of the estate.

Bankruptcy attorneys assist their clients, both individuals and corporations, in obtaining protection from creditors under existing bankruptcy laws and with financial reorganization and debt repayment.

Corporation lawyers advise corporations concerning their legal rights, obligations, or privileges. They study constitutions, statutes, previous decisions, ordinances, and decisions of quasi-judicial bodies that are applicable to corporations. They advise corporations on the pros and cons of prosecuting or defending a lawsuit. They act as agents of the corporation in various transactions and seek to keep clients from expensive litigation.

Maritime lawyers, sometimes referred to as *admiralty lawyers,* specialize in laws regulating commerce and navigation on the high seas and any navigable waters, including inland lakes and rivers. Although there is a general maritime law, it operates in each country according to that country's courts, laws, and customs. Maritime law covers contracts, insurance, property damage, and personal injuries.

Intellectual property lawyers focus on helping their clients with patents, trademarks, and copyright protection. *Patent lawyers* are intellectual property lawyers who specialize in securing patents for inventors from the United States Patent Office and prosecuting or defending suits of patent infringements. They prepare detailed specifications for the patent, may organize a corporation, or advise an existing corporation to commercialize on a patent. Biotechnology patent law is a further specialization of patent law. *Biotechnology patent lawyers* specialize in helping biotechnology researchers, scientists, and research corporations with all legal aspects of their biotechnology patents.

Elder law attorneys are lawyers who specialize in providing legal services for the elderly and, in some cases, the disabled.

Tax attorneys handle cases resulting from problems of inheritance, income tax, estate tax, franchises, and real estate tax, among other things.

Insurance attorneys advise insurance companies about legal matters pertaining to insurance transactions. They approve the wording of insurance policies, review the legality of claims against the company, and draw up legal documents.

International lawyers specialize in the body of rules that are observed by nations in their relations with one another. Some of these laws have been agreed to in treaties, some have evolved from long-standing customs and traditions.

Securities and exchange lawyers monitor individuals and corporations involved in trading and oversee their activities to make sure they comply with applicable laws. When corporations undergo takeovers and mergers, securities and exchange lawyers are there to represent the corporations' interests and fulfill all legal obligations involved in the transaction.

Real estate lawyers handle the transfer of property and perform such duties as searching public records and deeds to establish titles of property, holding funds for investment in escrow accounts, and acting as trustees of property. They draw up legal documents and act as agents in various real estate transactions.

Title attorneys deal with titles, leases, contracts, and other legal documents pertaining to the ownership of land, and gas, oil, and mineral rights. They prepare documents to cover the purchase or sale of such property and rights, examine documents to determine ownership, advise organizations about legal requirements concerning titles, and participate in the trial or lawsuits in connection with titles.

It is important to note that once you are licensed to practice law, you are legally qualified to practice any one or more of these and many other specialties. Some *general practitioners* handle both criminal and civil matters of all sorts. To become licensed, you must be admitted to the bar of that state. *Bar examiners* test the qualifications of applicants. They prepare and administer written exams covering legal subjects, examine candidates orally, and recommend admission of those who meet the prescribed standards.

Lawyers become judges by either election or appointment, and preside over federal, state, county, or municipal courts. Judges administer court procedures during trials and hearings and establish new rules on questions where standard procedures have not previously been set. They read or listen to claims made by parties involved in civil suits and make decisions based on facts, applicable statutes, and prior court decisions. They examine evidence in criminal cases to see if it supports the charges. Judges listen to the presentation of cases, rule on the admission of evidence and testimony, and settle disputes between attorneys. They instruct juries on their duties and advise them of laws that apply to the case. They sentence defendants found guilty of criminal charges and decide who is responsible in nonjury civil cases. Besides their work in the courtroom, judges also research legal matters, study prior rulings, write opinions, and keep abreast of legislation that may affect their rulings.

Some judges have other titles such as *magistrate,* or *justice,* and preside over a limited jurisdiction. Magistrates hear civil cases in which damages do not exceed a prescribed maximum, as well as minor misdemeanor cases that do not involve penitentiary sentences or fines that exceed a certain specified amount.

REQUIREMENTS
High School

A high school diploma, a college degree, and three years of law school are minimum requirements for a law degree. A high school diploma is a first step on the ladder of education that a lawyer must climb. If you are considering a career in law, courses such as government, history, social studies, and economics provide a solid background for entering college-level courses. Speech courses are also helpful to build strong communication skills necessary for the profession. Also take advantage of any computer-related classes or experience you can get, because lawyers and judges often use technology to research and interpret the law, from surfing the Internet to searching legal databases.

Postsecondary Training

To enter any law school approved by the American Bar Association, you must satisfactorily complete at least three, and usually four, years of college work. Most law schools do not specify any particular courses for prelaw education. Usually a liberal arts track is most advisable, with courses in English, history, economics, social sciences, logic, and public speaking. A college student planning on specialization in a particular area of law, however, might also take courses significantly related to that area, such as economics, agriculture, or political science. Those interested should write to several law schools to learn more about any requirements and to see if they will accept credits from the college the student is planning to attend.

Currently, over 185 law schools in the United States are approved by the American Bar Association; others, many of them night schools, are approved by state authorities only. Most of the approved law schools, however, do have night sessions to accommodate part-time students. Part-time courses of study usually take four years.

Law school training consists of required courses such as legal writing and research, contracts, criminal law, constitutional law, torts, and property. The second and third years may be devoted to specialized courses of interest to the student, such as evidence, business transactions and corporations, or admiralty. The study of cases and decisions is of basic importance to the law student, who will be required to read and study thousands of these cases. A degree of juris doctor (J.D.) or bachelor of laws (LL.B.) is usually granted upon graduation. Some law students considering specialization, research, or teaching may go on for advanced study.

Most law schools require that applicants take the Law School Admission Test (LSAT), where prospective law students are tested on their critical thinking, writing, and reasoning abilities.

Certification or Licensing

Every state requires that lawyers be admitted to the bar of that state before they can practice. They require that applicants graduate from an approved law school and that they pass a written examination in the state in which they intend to practice. In a few states, graduates of law schools within the state are excused from these written examinations. After lawyers have been admitted to the bar in one state, they can practice in another state without taking a written examination if the states have reciprocity agreements; however, they will be required to meet certain state standards of good character and legal experience and pay any applicable fees.

Other Requirements

Federal courts and agencies have their own rules regulating admission to practice. Other requirements vary among the states. For example, the states of Vermont, New York, Washington, Virginia, California, Maine, and Wyoming allow a person who has spent several years reading law in a law office but has no college training or who has a combination of reading and law school experience to take the state bar examination. Few people now enter law practice in this manner.

A few states accept the study of law by correspondence. Some states require that newly graduated lawyers serve a period of clerkship in an established law firm before they are eligible to take the bar examination.

Almost all judges appointed or elected to any court must be lawyers and members of the bar, usually with many years of experience.

Both lawyers and judges have to be effective communicators, work well with people, and be able to find creative solutions to problems, such as complex court cases.

EXPLORING

There are several ways you can find out more about what it is like to be a lawyer or judge. First, sit in on a trial or two at your local or state courthouse. Try to focus mainly on the judge and the lawyer and take note of what they do. Write down questions you have and terms or actions you do not understand. Then, talk to your guidance counselor and ask for help in setting up a telephone or in-person interview with a judge or lawyer. Ask questions and get the scoop on what those careers are really all about. Also, talk to your guidance counselor or political science teacher about starting or joining a shadowing program. Shadowing programs allow you to follow a person in a certain career around for a day or two to get an idea of what goes on in a typical day. You may even be invited to help out with a few minor duties.

You can also search the World Wide Web for general information about lawyers and judges and current court cases. Read court transcripts and summary opinions written by judges on issues of importance today. After you've done some research and talked to a lawyer or judge and you still think you are destined for law school, try to get a part-time job in a law office. Ask your guidance counselor for help.

If you are already in law school, you might consider becoming a student member of the American Library Association. Student members receive *Student Lawyer,* a magazine that contains useful information for aspiring lawyers. Sample articles from the magazine can be read at http://www.abanet.org/lsd/stulawyer.

EMPLOYERS

About 75 percent of practicing lawyers in the United States work in private practice, either in law firms or alone. The others are employed in government, often at the local level. Lawyers working for the federal government hold positions in the Departments of Justice, Treasury, and Defense. Lawyers also hold positions as house counsel for public utilities, transportation companies, banks, insurance companies, real estate agencies, manufacturing firms, welfare and religious organizations, and other businesses and nonprofit organizations.

Judges and magistrates work for federal, state, and local levels of government.

STARTING OUT

The first steps in entering the law profession are graduation from an approved law school and passing a state bar examination. Usually beginning lawyers do not go into solo practice right away. It is often difficult to become established, and additional experience is helpful to the beginning lawyer. Also, most lawyers do not specialize in a particular branch of law without first gaining experience. Beginning lawyers usually work as assistants to experienced lawyers. At first they do mainly research and routine work. After a few years of successful experience, they may be ready to go out on their own. Other choices open to the beginning lawyer include joining an established law firm or entering into partnership with another lawyer. Positions are also available with banks, business corporations, insurance companies, private utilities, and with a number of government agencies at different levels.

Many new lawyers are recruited by law firms or other employers directly from law school. Recruiters come to the school and interview possible hires. Other new graduates can get job leads from local and state bar associations.

ADVANCEMENT

Lawyers with outstanding ability can expect to go a long way in their profession. Novice lawyers generally start as law clerks, but as they prove themselves and develop their abilities, many opportunities for advancement will arise. They may be promoted to junior partner in a law firm or establish their own practice. Lawyers may enter politics and become judges, mayors, congressmen, or other government leaders. Top positions are available in business, too, for the qualified lawyer. Lawyers working for the federal government advance according to the civil service system. Judges usually advance from lower courts to higher courts either in terms of the matters that are decided or in terms of the level—local, state, or federal.

EARNINGS

Incomes generally increase as the lawyer gains experience and becomes better known in the field. The beginning lawyer in solo practice may barely make ends meet for the first few years. According to the National Association for Law Placement, 2002 median salaries for new lawyers ranged from $53,500 for lawyers employed by firms of two to 25 attorneys to $118,000 for lawyers employed by firms of 501 or more attorneys. Those working for the government made approximately $40,000. Starting salaries for lawyers in business were $60,000. Recent graduates entering private practice made the most, earning approximately $80,000.

Experienced lawyers earn salaries that vary depending on the type, size, and location of their employers. According to the U.S. Department of Labor, the 2002 median salary for practicing lawyers was $90,290, although some senior partners earned well over $1 million a year. Ten percent earned less than $44,490. Attorneys working for the federal government had median annual earnings of $98,790 in 2002. State and local government attorneys generally made less, earning $67,910 and $69,710, respectively, in 2002.

Judges earned median annual salaries of $94,070 in 2002, according to the U.S. Department of Labor. Salaries ranged from less than $24,250 to more than $138,300.

In 2002, the chief justice of the United States earned $198,600, while associate justices of the Supreme Court earned $190,100. A survey conducted by the National Center for State Courts reports the 2002 salary average for judges in the states' highest courts was $125,485. At the state level, judges serving in intermediate appellate courts averaged $116,064, and in general jurisdiction trial courts, earned an average of $109,811.

WORK ENVIRONMENT

Offices and courtrooms are usually pleasant, although busy, places to work. Lawyers also spend significant amounts of time in law libraries or record rooms, in the homes and offices of clients, and sometimes in the jail cells of clients or prospective witnesses. Many lawyers never work in a courtroom. Unless they are directly involved in litigation, they may never perform at a trial.

Some courts, such as small claims, family, or surrogate, may have evening hours to provide flexibility to the community. Criminal arraignments may be held at any time of the day or night. Court hours for most lawyers and judges are usually regular business hours, with a one-hour lunch break. Often lawyers have to work long hours, spending evenings and weekends preparing cases and materials and working with clients. In addition to the work, the lawyer must always keep up with the latest developments in the profession. Also, it takes a long time to become a qualified lawyer, and it may be difficult to earn an adequate living until the lawyer gets enough experience to develop an established private practice.

Lawyers who are employed at law firms must often work grueling hours to advance in the firm. Spending long weekend hours doing research and interviewing people should be expected.

OUTLOOK

According to the *Occupational Outlook Handbook*, employment for lawyers is expected to grow about as fast as the average through 2012, but record numbers of law school graduates have created strong competition for jobs. Continued population growth, typical business activities, and increased numbers of legal cases involving health care, environmental, intellectual property, international law, elder law, and sexual harassment issues, among others, will create a steady demand for lawyers. Law services will be more accessible to the middle-income public with the popularity of prepaid legal services and clinics. However, stiff competition has and will continue to urge lawyers to look elsewhere for jobs, in administrative, managerial, and business positions, where legal training is useful.

The top 10 percent of the graduating seniors of the country's best law schools will have more opportunities with well-known law firms and jobs on legal staffs of corporations, in government agencies, and in law schools in the next few decades. Lawyers in solo practice will find it hard to earn a living until their practice is fully established. The best opportunities exist in small towns or suburbs of large cities, where there is less competition and new lawyers can meet potential clients more easily.

Graduates with lower class standings and from lesser known schools may have difficulty in obtaining the most desirable positions. Banks, insurance companies, real estate firms, government agencies, and other organizations often hire law graduates. Legal positions in the armed forces are also available.

Employment of judges is expected to grow more slowly than the average through 2012. Judges who retire, however, will need to be replaced. There may be an increase in judges in cities with large population growth, but competition will be high for any openings.

TO LEARN MORE ABOUT LAWYERS AND JUDGES

BOOKS

Abrams, Lisa L. *The Official Guide to Legal Specialties.* Orlando, Fla.: Harcourt, 2000.

Echaore-McDavid, Susan. *Career Opportunities in Law and the Legal Industry.* New York: Facts On File, 2002.

Hall, Kermit, ed. *Oxford Guide to United States Supreme Court Decisions.* New York: Oxford University Press, 2001.

Irons, Peter H., and Howard Zinn. *A People's History of the Supreme Court.* New York: Penguin, 2000.

Miller, Robert H. *Law School Confidential: A Complete Guide to the Law School Experience.* Irvine, Calif.: Griffin, 2000.

Noyes, Shanna Connell, and Henry S. Noyes. *Acing Your First Year of Law School: The Ten Steps to Success You Won't Learn in Class.* Buffalo, N.Y.: William S. Hein & Co., 1999.

ORGANIZATIONS

For information about law student services offered by the ABA, contact

American Bar Association (ABA)
Service Center
541 North Fairbanks Court
Chicago, IL 60611
Tel: 312-988-5522
Email: service@abanet.org
http://www.abanet.org

For information on workshops and seminars, contact
Association of American Law Schools
1201 Connecticut Avenue, NW, Suite 800
Washington, DC 20036-2605
Tel: 202-296-8851
Email: aals@aals.org
http://www.aals.org

The FBA provides information for lawyers and judges involved in federal practice.

Federal Bar Association (FBA)
Student Services
2215 M Street, NW
Washington, DC 20037
Tel: 202-785-1614
Email: fba@fedbar.org
http://fedbar.org

For information on choosing a law school, law careers, salaries, and alternative law careers, contact

National Association for Law Placement
1025 Connecticut Avenue, NW, Suite 1110
Washington, DC 20036-5413
Tel: 202-835-1001
Email: info@nalp.org
http://www.nalp.org

TO LEARN MORE ABOUT WILLIAM H. REHNQUIST

BOOKS

Dean, John W. *The Rehnquist Choice: The Untold Story of the Nixon Appointment that Redefined the Supreme Court.* New York: Simon & Schuster, 2001.

Lazarus, Edward. *Closed Chambers: The Rise, Fall and Future of the Modern Supreme Court.* New York: Penguin Books, 1999.

Rehnquist, William H. *The Supreme Court.* New York: Vintage Books, 2002.

Schwartz, Bernard. *A History of the Supreme Court.* New York: Oxford University Press, 1993.

Yarbrough, Tinsley E. *The Rehnquist Court and the Constitution.* New York: Oxford University Press, 2000.

ARTICLES

"All Politics." *CNN.com.* Available online. URL: http://www.cnn.com/ALLPOLITICS/1997/gen/resources/ players/rehnquist/. Posted March 3, 1997.

"Rehnquist." *Biography on A&E* website. Available online. URL: http://www.biography.com/search/article.jsp?aid = 9454479. Posted 2000.

"Split Ruling on Affirmative Action." *NPR.org.* Available online. URL:http://www.npr.org/news/specials/michigan/index. html. Posted June 23, 2003.

"William H. Rehnquist." Supreme Court Historical Society. Available online. http://www.supremecourthistory.org/ myweb/justice/rehnquist.htm. Posted March 2, 2000.

Bacon, Perry Jr. "And the Winner Is . . . Affirmative Action." *Time Magazine.* Available online. URL: http://www. time.com/time/nation/article/0,8599,460435,00.html. Posted June 23, 2003.

Greenhouse, Linda. "Bush v. Gore: A Special Report; Election Case a Test and a Trauma for Justices." *New York Times,* February 20, 2001.

Greenhouse, Linda. "Court Says States Need Not Finance Divinity Studies." *New York Times,* February 26, 2004.

Greenhouse, Linda. "In a Momentous Term, Justices Remake the Law, and the Court." *New York Times,* July 1, 2003.

Jenkins, John A. "The Partisan: A Talk with Justice Rehnquist." *New York Times Magazine.* March 3, 1985.

Rehnquist, William H. "Remarks of the Chief Justice: American Meteorological Society." Supreme Court of the United States website. Available online. URL: http://www.supremecourtus.gov/publicinfo/speeches/sp_10-23-01.html. Posted October 23, 2001.

Stevenson, Richard W. "The President's Acquittal: The Chief Justice; Rehnquist Goes With the Senate Flow, 'Wiser, but Not a Sadder Man.'" *New York Times,* February 13, 1999.

Taylor, Stuart. "More Vigor for the Right; Court Would Ease Toward Conservatism Without Abruptly Changing in Direction." *New York Times,* June 18, 1986.

WEBSITES

PBS Online: Supreme Court Watch

http://www.pbs.org/newshour/bb/law/supreme_court

Supreme Court Historical Society

http://www.supremecourthistory.org

U.S. Supreme Court Multimedia

http://www.oyez.org

INDEX

Page numbers in *italics* indicate illustrations.

ABOUT THE AUTHOR

Scott Cameron specializes in educational books and television programs for children and adults. He has written seven children's books and has written and edited numerous high school and college textbooks. He is also an educational content specialist for companies such as Sesame Workshop, where he has helped develop curricula for international versions of *Sesame Street*. Mr. Cameron has been an instructor and teacher trainer in Japan and the United States. He holds a master's degree in education from Columbia University.